GREAT

DISCOVER THE GREAT PLAINS
Series editor: Richard Edwards, Center for Great Plains Studies

DAVID J. WISHART

PLAINS

Indians

UNIVERSITY OF NEBRASKA PRESS   *Lincoln and London*

A Project of the Center for Great Plains Studies, University of Nebraska

∞

Library of Congress
Cataloging-in-Publication Data
Names: Wishart, David J., 1946– author.
Title: Great Plains Indians / David J. Wishart.
Description: Lincoln: University of Nebraska
Press, 2016. | Series: Discover the Great Plains |
Includes bibliographical references and index.
Identifiers: LCCN 2015044945
ISBN 9780803269620 (pbk: alk. paper)
ISBN 9780803290938 (epub)
ISBN 9780803290945 (mobi)
ISBN 9780803290952 (pdf)
Subjects: LCSH: Indians of North America—
Great Plains—History. | Great Plains—History.
Classification: LCC E78.G73 W55 2016 |
DDC 978.004/97—dc23 LC record available
at http://lccn.loc.gov/2015044945

Set in Garamond Premier by M. Scheer.
Designed by N. Putens.

CONTENTS

ILLUSTRATIONS

ACKNOWLEDGMENTS

I would like to thank Richard Edwards, director of the Center for Great Plains Studies at the University of Nebraska–Lincoln, for suggesting this project to me and for supporting the production of the maps and the acquisition of the photographs. My thanks also go to Ezra Zeitler of the Department of Geography, University of Wisconsin-Eau Claire for creating the maps, to Jessica Ditmore for putting the manuscript into a form suitable for submission, and to Joshua Caster, archives manager at the University of Nebraska–Lincoln, for photographing images. I am, as always, grateful to Bridget Barry for her sound advice and considerate editing of the initial manuscript and to Joeth Zucco for doing such a fine job of the copyediting. My wife, Sarah Disbrow, helped greatly by listening as I worked the book out aloud. Finally, I would like to say that it was an honor to write this book on Plains Indians and to play a small role in keeping their histories alive.

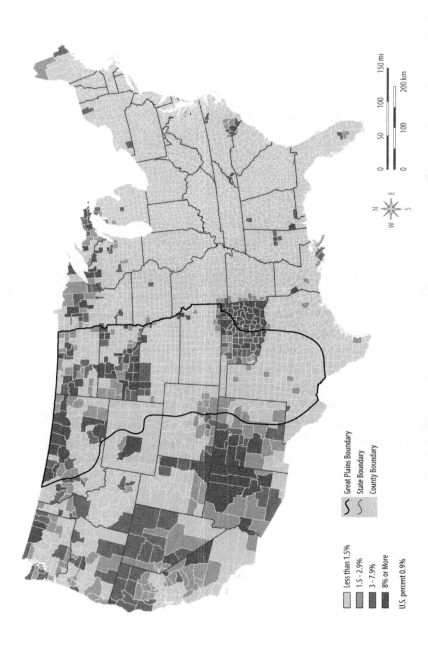

INTRODUCTION

Plains Indians in the 2010 Census

On the census map showing the distribution of American Indians and Alaska Natives in the United States in 2010, the Great Plains stands out (fig. 1). The map locates those Americans who identified as being American Indian or Alaska Native *alone* in the 2010 census. If those who reported being American Indian and Alaska Native in combination with other races—an option in the census since 2000—are counted, then the total numbers would just about double, though the geographic concentrations would remain much the same. In the continental United States, only the Southwest matches the Great Plains as an Indian region, however measured.

The census map shows two distinct belts of Indians in the American Great Plains. On the northern Great Plains, the populations of many counties within, or around, reservations are more than 8 percent Indian. Many other counties nearby are 3 to 7.9 percent Indian. (By comparison, 0.9 percent of the population of the United States as a whole is Indian alone.)

1. American Indians in the contiguous United States as a percentage of county population, 2010. Source: U.S. Census Bureau, 2012. Created by Ezra J. Zeitler.

The reservations of the northern Plains are what remain of the Indians' land base following the wholesale dispossession of the nineteenth century. Some of the largest reservations in the country, by both area and population, are here (fig. 2). Pine Ridge, home of the Oglala Sioux (or Lakota), has the second highest Indian alone population (16,906) of any reservation in the country, and adjacent Rosebud Reservation (Brule Sioux), with 9,809 Indians, ranks third. All together, the Sioux nation, both on and off reservations, is the third largest tribal grouping in the United States, with an Indian alone population of 112,176. The Blackfeet Reservation of northern Montana, with an Indian alone population of 9,149 in 2010, also makes the top ten list of most populous reservations. Much of the northern Great Plains is still Indian.

The same can be said about Oklahoma, the second concentration of Indians in the Great Plains, although there the Indian population is more integrated, culturally and geographically, than those on the northern reservations. Almost all the counties in the eastern third of Oklahoma are more than 8 percent Indian; in fact, of the 187 counties in the United States (including Alaska) that fall into this category, 55 are in Oklahoma. Only the Oklahoma Panhandle has a negligible Indian presence.

The reason there are so many Indians in Oklahoma (321,687 in 2010, second only to California) is that this was Indian Territory in the nineteenth century, the last place to put Indians from elsewhere in the Great Plains and the nation when their lands were taken by Americans. Reservations in the former Indian Territory, with the exception of the Osage Reservation, which still exists today, were extinguished in the build-up to statehood in 1907. Oklahoma Indians are now enumerated by the census bureau and administered by tribal governments in Tribal Jurisdictional Statistical Areas,

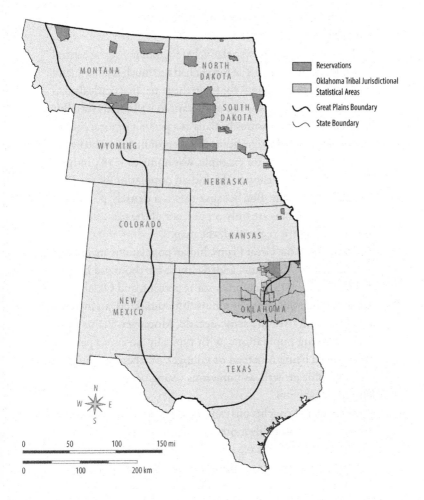

2. American Indian reservations on the Great Plains, 2010. Source: U.S. Census Bureau, 2010. Created by Ezra J. Zeitler.

whose boundaries approximate those of the former reservations (fig. 2).

The census map shows relatively few Indians in the central Great Plains and Texas. The former had too much rich farmland to remain in Indian hands for long; the latter, in its early days as the Texas Republic, was too intolerant to let Indians stay. But because the map measures Indians as a percent of total county populations, it hides significant numbers of Indians who live in urban areas. Denver, for example, was home to 13,184 Indians in 2013, almost as many as the Indian population of the Pine Ridge Reservation. But because this is a densely populated urban area, Indians are only 0.5 percent of the total, and they do not, therefore, register on the map.

Throughout the Great Plains, Indian populations are increasing rapidly. South Dakota added almost ten thousand Indians from 2000 to 2010, an increase of 15 percent, and Oklahoma's Indian population grew by almost fifty thousand, an increase of 18 percent, over the same decade. Moreover, Plains Indians are young populations, with typically 40 or 50 percent of the total being nineteen or younger. So there is a built-in demographic growth, as numerous young people advance to childbearing years.

A number of conclusions can be drawn from the census data. First, there are probably more Indians on the Great Plains now than at any time in the past. Second, Indians will only become a larger and larger proportion of Great Plains populations in the future. Such a scenario would have seemed inconceivable in 1900, when most Plains Indian populations bottomed out.

A third conclusion revealed in the census data is that the majority of Plains Indians are poor. Certainly, there are Plains Indians who have succeeded in all walks of American life, and are prosperous, but they are exceptions to the pervasive poverty. Six of the eleven poorest counties in the United States, as measured by per capita income, lie within or overlap reservations on the northern Great Plains. In fact, these six places of abject poverty are Sioux reservations in North Dakota and South Dakota, with the Crow Creek Reservation in central South Dakota being the poorest of the poor. Many other northern Plains reservations are on the unenviable list of the nation's hundred poorest counties, including Big Horn County in Montana, which overlaps the Crow reservation; Rolette County in North Dakota, where the Chippewa's Turtle Mountain Reservation is located; and Thurston County, Nebraska, which includes the Winnebago and Omaha Reservations.

Behind these cold, hard statistics are the harsh realities of the conditions of poverty: high unemployment rates (often 70 percent or more); epidemics of alcoholism, violence, suicides, obesity, and diabetes; inadequate housing in a region of climatic extremes; and lack of access to health services, or even to fresh fruits and vegetables. Such dire living conditions result in low life expectancies. On the Pine Ridge Reservation, life expectancy at birth for a male is estimated to be forty-eight years and for a female fifty-two years; by comparison, Haiti, the poorest country in the Western Hemisphere, has life expectancies of sixty and sixty-four for males and females respectively.

This short book travels a long road in an attempt to explain how Plains Indians have come to this point in time. The account begins more than thirteen thousand years ago with the initial settlement of the Great Plains from Asia and relates how these first Americans lived for millennia as hunters and gatherers in physical environments that were always changing. The pace of change accelerated with the incursion of Europeans after A D 1500, bringing guns, horses, and epidemic diseases that changed Indian lives forever. The story then halts, and, in a transection through time, presents a historical geography of Indian life on the Great Plains on the eve of the American takeover in 1803.

It moves ahead again and explains how the Plains Indians lost most of their lands and much of their traditional cultures in a tumultuous century of dispossession. The final chapter shows that dispossession continued after 1900, but it also reveals that Indian populations rebounded and rights were asserted, changing the tenor of the story from a tragedy of loss into a triumph of survival, with, perhaps, the prospect of a better future ahead.

GREAT PLAINS INDIANS

CHAPTER ONE

Since Time Immemorial

No one is absolutely indigenous; no one just grew out of the ground, though many Native American accounts say that is indeed what happened. But longevity in a place—time to sink deep roots, time to belong there—is its own form of indigenousness. Americans, who took control of most of the Great Plains with the Louisiana Purchase of 1803, are clearly the newcomers to the region. Europeans go back further, to Spaniard Francisco Vásquez de Coronado in 1541, wandering lost across the High Plains of Texas, Oklahoma, and Kansas. But even five hundred years or so are just a drop in the ocean of time compared to Plains Indians, whose ultimate ancestors were in the Great Plains for sure by 13,500 BP (Before Present), and almost certainly much earlier.

Origins

There is much disagreement about when and how the first peoples came into the Great Plains. Most fundamentally, there is disagreement between the Indians' own accounts of their origins and modern-day scholars' explanations of early Indian settlement. It's hard to see how these conflicting interpretations can ever be reconciled because they are products of such different world views, though in some ways the two sets of stories complement each other.

In the Blackfeet creation story, for example, Napi (Old Man) working northward in what is now Montana and Alberta, made the mountains, the prairies, and the birds and animals. He laid down the Milk River and raised the Sweet Grass Hills above the surrounding prairie. Then he made people, shaping them from clay, and he showed them how to survive by hunting animals and gathering herbs and berries. He demonstrated to the people how to make fire and cook the meat of the animals they had killed. He told how knowledge would come to them through animals in dreams that would guide them in their daily lives. Old Man kept moving north, to the Porcupine Hills and almost as far as the Red Deer River, making people as he went and providing them with herds of bison. He showed the people how to take the bison by driving them over cliffs and how to use stone tools to cut the meat and skin the hides for use as shelter. His work done, Old Man disappeared into the mountains, but not before he had reassured the people, the Blackfeet, that he would take care of them and someday return.

This story of origins, and many others like it throughout the Great Plains, tell much about traditional Indian life: subsistence by hunting and gathering from a broad spectrum of the environment; a deep, spiritual attachment to place (the Sweet Grass Hills are still a sacred place to the Blackfeet); the vitality of the dream world, informing the waking world; the irrelevance of linear time, because, as the Kiowa poet and novelist N. Scott Momaday explained, Indians inhabited an "extended present," a "dimension of timelessness" where "all things happen." And in ceremonies, meticulously relayed from generation to generation, Indians retold the story of their origins, giving it an immediacy and allowing them to be participants in their ongoing creation story.

By contrast, modern scholars' accounts of Indian origins are all about time, and there is much disagreement here too.

0   CM   5

0   INCHES   2

3. Clovis spear point. Courtesy of the Nebraska State Historical Society.

For more than half a century, a single explanation, the theory of Clovis culture, dominated scientific understanding of the original colonization of the Americas. The theory was based initially on archaeological excavations at Blackwater Draw, near Clovis, New Mexico, which revealed elegantly fluted stone spear points alongside the bones of mammoths and other now-extinct large mammals, all dating to about 13,000 BP (fig. 3). Scores of other archeological sites identified as Clovis have been found throughout the Great Plains from Alberta to Texas. At one of these sites, Anzick, in western Montana, archaeologists uncovered the remains of a boy aged about two, painted with red ochre and layered with Clovis artifacts.

Archeologists inferred from their painstaking work that the people of Clovis culture were big-game hunters who had migrated across the Bering Strait during the waning stages of the last (Wisconsin) glaciation, when sea levels were much lower than now, and a wide causeway connected Siberia and Alaska. According to the theory, the hunters followed their prey south along an ice-free corridor that traced the eastern front of the Rockies, between the descending mountain glaciers and the massive continental, or Laurentide, ice sheet. This was not a migration as such, because Clovis people could not have had a destination in mind; rather, it was a territorial expansion following the game through a formidable post-glacial landscape of marshes, rocky outcrops, and icy raging rivers. Within the short span of a few hundred years, the theory goes, Clovis people, a single, successful hunting culture, had thinly populated the continental United States. This story of ultimate American origins became entrenched.

As the horizon of archaeological research widened, though, Clovis theory became less persuasive. Evidence of a more ancient human presence in the Americas was found in sites from Wisconsin to Chile. It seemed increasingly likely that a preexisting population was in place when Clovis people arrived. After all, the migration route across the Bering Strait land bridge had been available for much of the sixty thousand years of the Wisconsin glaciation. When the late-glacial migration of the Clovis peoples took place, the established residents may have readily adopted the superior hunting technology (the efficient spear points) of the newcomers. There has long been what geographer Carl O. Sauer called "an ingrained bias of setting up short calendars for the New World," and surely this begrudging time scale will continue to be extended back as new archeological discoveries are made and new methods of analysis open up new horizons of discovery.

The excavations at Clovis sites, and other sites of similar age, show that the early Great Plains hunters preyed on a wide range of large animals—mammoths, mastodons, horses, bison, camels, and more—as well as an array of small game. The presence of bone and ivory sewing needles at many of these sites, and of the spurred tools that drilled the eyes in them, is evidence of the manufacture of hide clothes and boots, which enabled survival in a waning glacial world where winters were much more severe than now.

But these sites conceal as much as they reveal. Much of the potential evidence of food gathering has long since decomposed into the earth. If the subsistence patterns of more recent hunters on the Great Plains (such as the Blackfeet, Crows, and Sioux) are any guideline, then food collection, probably by women, would also have been a foundation of subsistence for the first inhabitants. In fact, it may have been the most reliable source of food: roots, berries, and nuts grew in known places at known times of the year and were easier to take than elusive animals.

Of course, the archaeological sites, incisions into a vanished world, tell little about the innermost thinking of these first peoples—how they loved, how they treated each other, how they hoped and feared, how they explained their very existence, all those things that add up to being human.

This was not at all an unchanging world. The natural world changed of its own accord. Climate continued to warm at the end of the Wisconsin glaciation until about 7000 BP (depending on the location), then began a long-term cooling process, though with many short-term fluctuations. Plains vegetation, striving to keep up with the changing climate, went from tundra immediately after the withdrawal of the ice sheets, to prairie grasslands in warm and dry periods, and forest in warm and wet times. At the time of Clovis culture, for example, spruce forests grew over much of the northern Great Plains. And 5000 years ago, the Wyoming plains, now a semiarid grassland, were covered by an open woodland of massive cedar trees, interspersed with junipers and ponderosa pines. These environmental changes would not have been discernable in a single lifetime, but over the course of generations humans had to adapt, just like the animals they depended upon.

Humans changed the natural world too, perhaps drastically. Their use of fire to drive game favored grassland plants, which regenerate from protected buds after each burning; whereas trees, especially seedlings and saplings, are destroyed in the process. More directly, hunters, with fire and sharp stone-tipped spears at their disposal, may well have had the capacity to eliminate many genera of large mammals. This theory of "Pleistocene overkill" has been advanced at least since the 1950s and has been at the center of a persistent paleoecological debate ever since.

Between 11,200 BP and 10,000 BP, after Clovis hunters entered the Great Plains, some thirty-five genera of mainly large mammals became extinct. The last evidence of mammoths in the United States has been dated to 10,900 BP. Also disappearing rapidly from the face of the American earth were varieties of slow-moving giant sloths (surely an easy target for hunters), horses, four-horned antelopes, beavers that weighed more than three hundred pounds, single-hump camels, and spruce-eating mastodons. Predators that lived on these browsers and grazers, such as saber-toothed cats, dire wolves, and the massive, ferocious short-faced bear, disappeared too. Significantly, no large North American mammals have become extinct since that time, though bison came close in the late 1880s.

Scholars like Sauer, and after him geoscientist Paul Martin, strenuously argued this overkill explanation, emphasizing the capacity of hunters, working cooperatively, to drive large mammals to extinction. Sauer, for example, explained how a fast-moving fire drive would particularly kill pregnant females and calves, striking right at the reproductive capacity of the herds. Sauer also emphasized that fire drives over cliffs, and the subsequent dispatch of injured and panic-stricken animals with spears, would have killed far more animals than could be used by the hunters.

The ecologist E. C. Pielou adds an interesting twist to the overkill thesis. Twelve genera of grazers and browsers that became extinct—camels, llamas, two types of deer, two types of pronghorns (a type of antelope), stag-moose, shrub-oxen, woodland musk-oxen, mastodons, mammoths, and horses—had been in North America for millions of years before Clovis hunters arrived. Pielou argues that these animals had not learned to survive alongside such determined predators, and they were therefore eliminated. The large grazers and browsers that did survive, and which persist into the present—one species of bison (*Bison bison*), moose, elk, caribou, deer, mountain goat, and bighorn sheep—were, like the hunters, relatively recent migrants from Asia, where they had learned to co-exist with the human hunters.

Opponents of the overkill theory are just as certain in their arguments. They reason that mass extinctions had happened before, at least six times in the previous ten million years, some associated with the end of glaciations, and long before human hunters appeared on the scene. Moreover, their arguments go, Clovis peoples and their contemporaries were too few in number to eliminate entire populations of animals. These opponents of the human agency explanation emphasize instead the effects of climate change at the end of the Wisconsin glaciation and the associated disruption of habitats. For example, as the climate warmed and dried, tallgrass prairie that had supported horses, camels, and mammoths gave way to shortgrass prairie, which could not sustain them. Bison, however, favored the shortgrasses and flourished. Or to give another example, the evolving warm, dry climate led to a retreat of the spruce forests, and mastodons lost their preferred food and edged toward extinction.

The debate rages on and may never be resolved. A combination of human and environmental factors may be the most satisfactory answer. One thing is sure: these first Plains Indians lived in a world that changed substantially in a relatively short time. The ranks of large animals suitable for hunting thinned, leaving bison (and many smaller animals) as the Indians' staff of life for the next ten thousand years. Pondering this radically changed world, Pielou offered this evocative thought: "It is tempting to speculate on how many generations of human children marveled at stories of their forefathers' mammoth-hunting exploits and of their encounters with saber tooths. We shall never know."

Persistence and Change

For more than ten thousand years after Clovis culture, hundreds of generations of pedestrian hunters lived their (to us) anonymous lives in the vast expanses of the Great Plains. Archaeologists differentiate these people mainly by the distinctive shapes of their chipped stone projection points and tools. So Folsom peoples followed Clovis and occupied the Great Plains (and only the Great Plains) until 10,000 BP, to be followed in turn by Plano peoples, who persisted until about 7000 BP, and then by what is called the Archaic Period, which on the northern Great Plains (the chronology is different for the central and southern Great Plains) lasted until about 1500 BP.

These early pioneers, mobile hunter-gatherers living in small multifamily groups, left widespread but scant evidence of their existence on the Great Plains landscape. There are scattered campsites with basin-shaped fire pits filled with stones that held the heat for cooking and caches of stone tools and weapons, animal bones, and grinding stones, the latter indicating the importance of plant collection and preparation. There are tipi rings, small circles of stones that were used to hold down the sides of conical skin shelters, often found singly or in groups on defensible ridgetops. There are quarries throughout the region where Indians mined particularly favored deposits like the jasper of the Solomon and Republican River valleys, or the molasses-colored flint of the Knife River valley. Often expertly fashioned ancient artifacts are found hundreds of miles from their geological source.

There are also kill sites, such as the cliff at Head-Smashed-In, in southeastern Alberta, where six thousand years of bison bones are layered in the earth. There is rock art drawn and etched on cave and canyon walls, often depicting hunting scenes that evoke the close spiritual connection between humans and animals. Sometimes, as at the Dead Indian site in northwestern Wyoming, where mule deer skulls and antlers were found in deliberate arrangement, there is evidence of the ceremonial activity that consecrated everyday life. And there are the skeletal remains of humans themselves, sometimes brought to the surface by the farmer's plow. The visible evidence may well be scant, but right under our wheat fields and city streets, just below our feet, lie the bones of hundreds of generations of Plains Indians, slowly turning into soil, then geology, still belonging to the place.

Although the pedestrian hunters drew from a broad range of plants and animals for their subsistence, bison were the primary resource for most of this long period of time. They were driven over cliffs, as at Head-Smashed-In, and as taught to the Blackfeet by Old Man. At the Olsen-Chubbuck site near Kit Carson, Colorado, for example, hunters (a Plano culture from nine thousand to seven thousand years ago) stampeded bison into an arroyo, where they were killed at will. When the site was excavated in the 1950s, the skeletons of 190 bison (the now extinct *Bison occidentalis*) were found in layers. The bottom layer of bison, showing twisted spines from the fall, were not touched, suggesting (as Sauer argued) that more were killed than were needed. The middle layer was only partially butchered, but the bison in the top layer had been methodically cut up and the meat stacked into separate piles. The presence of scattered tongue remains across the site suggests that the hunters ate this delicacy as they worked. It was arduous work, but well worth the effort: a single adult bison could yield as much as four hundred pounds of meat, to be eaten fresh or else dried, mixed with fat and berries, and stored in hide containers for future use (the practice began after about 5000 BP). Add to this nutritious prairie turnips that the women collected in May and June, wild plums and chokecherries that grew in profusion, the beans of ground-nuts and hog peanuts, black walnuts from valley woodlands, and many other tubers, nuts, seeds, and fruits, and here was a sustaining diet.

The distinguished anthropologist Waldo Wedel once posed the question: Could pedestrian hunters have permanently occupied the High Plains, the expanse of flat uplands from Nebraska to Texas which then, as now, is characterized by seasonal extremes of climate, vast spaces, and a shortage of both water and timber? Wedel answered his own question in the affirmative: the essential resources—bison, water, and timber—were available, and the two main problems—harsh winters and sheer distance—could be overcome.

Except in protracted periods of drought, when they retreated to the margins of the Great Plains, bison were ubiquitous. They ranged widely in large herds in spring, summer, and early fall, and gathered in smaller herds in sheltered valleys in winter. In addition to furnishing fresh and dried meat, hides for tipi covers and clothes, robes for winter warmth, tendons for thread to stitch clothes and tipis, bones for awls, and much more, bison were also a source of fluids. Their bladders were used as water containers, their blood was drunk in times of water shortage, and the digesting grass in their stomachs could be squeezed to yield juices. Other animals such as pronghorns and mule deer were killed for food too.

There were three sources of water on the High Plains. First, the Arkansas and South Platte Rivers, which were fed by dependable Rocky Mountain snowmelt, could be relied upon as a year-long water source. But even smaller rivers and streams, which were dry much of the year, had occasional pools, or "raises," where the water table intersected the surface. Dry streambeds could even be dug into to find buried water that flowed silently between the sandy grains. There were also many springs along valley sides, where the Ogallala Aquifer, perhaps running along the top of an impervious bed of rock, emerged into the daylight. These springs were particularly abundant in eastern Colorado and southwestern Nebraska, and without a doubt the Indians knew them all. Finally, there were the innumerable depressions (later called "buffalo wallows" by American settlers) that pocked the surface of the High Plains and filled with ephemeral water after a rain or a snowmelt. Together, Wedel concluded, they provided an obtainable resource, with few places more than ten miles from water.

Trees, of course, were scarce on the High Plains, yet the Indians needed poles for their tipis and the travois (triangular frames) they constructed for haulage. But lodgepole pines, a favored source for large tipi poles, were available in fringing mountains like the Laramie Range in Wyoming and the Black Hills in South Dakota, and smaller poles could be cut from junipers that grew in the breaks of the plains, as in the canyon and mesa country of southeastern Colorado. The problem of fuel was solved, as it would be for American settlers in the 1880s, by "buffalo chips," dried bison dung.

The distances between the scattered water sources and to the migrating bison herds were spanned by using dogs as beasts of burden. Dogs could carry up to fifty pounds on their backs in pack saddles and haul seventy-five pounds (amounting to a small tipi cover, poles, and stakes) on a travois. They could transport such loads as far as ten miles a day, permitting the camps to be moved between the vital sources of water.

The Indians could not have stayed on the exposed uplands of the High Plains in winter, because it is a raw place of frigid temperatures and driving blizzards. But just to the west, where the High Plains drop toward the Rocky Mountains, are sheltered river valleys that provided water and sanctuary for Indians and bison alike. Chinooks, descending warm winds from the Rockies that melt the winter snow, would have been an asset too. The Big Timbers, a river bottom woodland along the Arkansas River in southeastern Colorado, was a particularly favored winter site right through to the last days of Indian independence, and so too was cloistered Purgatory Canyon, in the same general area, with its rock shelters and rock art standing out on the landscape as evidence of thousands of years of use.

Over those thousands of years, the fundamental patterns of Indian life on the Great Plains showed more continuity than change. Even given the short- and long-term climate swings that the Indians had to adjust to, life was predictable, a repeating cycle from dawn to dawn and spring to spring. Certainly life was predictable compared to what would come later after the arrival of Europeans and Americans.

Innovations were made for sure, such as better hunting techniques or more effective (or more decorative) forms of pottery, as would be expected from thinking, intelligent people. Innovations also filtered in from distant places. The atlatl, for example, a shaft that attached to the end of a spear and, acting as a lever, allowed the weapon to be thrown faster and farther, came into the Great Plains about 7500 BP. Later, about 2000 BP, the bow and arrow diffused south from the Arctic down through the region, greatly increasing the Indians' hunting efficiency.

The most important diffusion, however, as far as diversifying and securing the food base goes, was agriculture, which first appeared in the river valleys of the central and eastern Great Plains about one thousand years ago.

This extension of farming from the east was allowed by the benevolent climatic conditions that prevailed from AD 950 to 1250. Warm, moist air masses that originated over the Gulf of Mexico brought increased rainfall and a longer growing season to the eastern parts of what are now Kansas, Nebraska, and the Dakotas. Substantial village settlements were established in the Solomon and Republican River valleys of Kansas and Nebraska and in the middle Missouri River valley between the mouths of the White and Cheyenne tributaries. These were farming Indians, growing corn (the outer reach of a long diffusion wave that had started about six thousand years earlier in southeastern Mexico, where corn was first domesticated), beans, and squash. The agricultural villagers also hunted bison and other animals and collected the bounty of wild plants that the region had to offer. The settlements would wax and wane over the years, following the vicissitudes of climate, but this geographic distinction (more accurately a gradation) between the farming and hunting Indians of the eastern Great Plains and the exclusively bison hunters of the western Great Plains would still be evident when the United States took control of the region in 1803.

The advent of farming brought about a new, more fixed settlement pattern, as well as an enriched ceremonial life that revolved around the growth cycle of the crops, especially corn. The farmers of the Solomon and Republican River valleys, for example, lived in small villages, each composed of about ten large (thirty by twenty feet) rectangular earth lodges, housing in total about a hundred people. The villages were located on river terraces, where there was rich alluvial soil to cultivate and water and timber nearby. The remains found in storage pits and elsewhere at these sites show that the Indians had a diversified subsistence base. Bison scapula (shoulder) hoes, shelled corn, and charred beans and squash attest to their farming activities; while bison and elk bones, walnut-stained grinding stones, hackberry and sunflower seeds, and piles of freshwater mussel shells stand as evidence of their continued hunting and gathering. The presence of Upper Republican (this is the name given to this early farming society) pottery and other artifacts in distant places, such as eastern Wyoming, suggests that the Indians still made communal bison hunts far out into the Great Plains and also raises the likely possibility that even at this early date, trade networks spanned the region. Large cemeteries showing long durations of use were located on the river terraces near the villages, adding yet another deep connection to the homeland. These Upper Republican farming villages persisted until about AD 1300, when cooler, drier climatic conditions led to their decline and abandonment. It is possible, though not proven, that these first Great Plains farmers were the ancestors of the historic Pawnees, a powerful farming and hunting people who dominated the country from the Loup River in Nebraska to the Arkansas River in Oklahoma at the time Americans arrived on the scene.

A similar sequence of growth and decline took place in the middle Missouri River valley, also calibrated to the swings in climate. By AD 900 at least thirty-five villages lined the banks of the Missouri River, just above and below the present-day site of Pierre, South Dakota. A second concentration of villages along the Missouri River emerged by AD 1100 to the north and south of where Bismarck, North Dakota, is now located. As in the Upper Republican system, these were rectangular earth lodge villages situated on river terraces. But the Missouri River villages were fortified, unlike those along the Solomon and

Republican Rivers, suggesting that the bison hunters may have coveted their corn-filled caches. These villages also diminished, or disappeared altogether, with the climatic reversals after A D 1250. But they would revive in more favorable conditions after A D 1500 and continue in an unbroken sequence through to the historic villages of the Mandan and Hidatsa Indians.

But by then, there was another factor, a new cause of change, in the universe of the Plains Indians: the wide world came trickling, then crashing in, and Indian lives would never be the same again.

The European Impact

If Indians had been accustomed to dividing time into linear segments, then the cardinal division of their histories might well have been designated B E and A E : Before Europeans and After Europeans. Beginning in the mid-1500s on the southern Great Plains and in the late 1600s on the northern Great Plains, Europeans moved in and transformed the Indians' enduring world into a place of tumult and uncertainty.

Spain was the first of the European powers to extend its imperial reach into the Great Plains, but it was a tentative reach that failed to take hold (fig. 4). Spaniards were drawn north from Mexico to the Upper Rio Grande valley in 1540, seeking gold to plunder and souls to save. The following year, Coronado led his expedition across the southern High Plains, looking for the mythical golden villages of Quivira (but finding only the grass huts of the Wichitas in present-day Kansas). The journals of the expedition (with Europeans came the first written reports on the Great Plains and its inhabitants) described a fertile grassland of great agricultural potential, inhabited by pedestrian Indians who greeted the Spaniards without fear or hostility (or even a show of surprise). But in reality, there was little there to attract the Spaniards: there were no precious metals, the Indians were too decentralized to be useful as labor, and the vast distances were intimidating. The best use of the region for Spain was to serve as a barrier in the way of French, British, and eventually American advance from the east.

Even if Spain had wanted to colonize the Great Plains, it would have been unable to do so because by the middle of the eighteenth century the Comanches had established their own empire in the grasslands through war, trade manipulation, and shrewd diplomacy, an empire that would last for more than a hundred years. This underscores an important issue that is too easily overlooked when considering the implications of the European and American advances into the Great Plains: the Indians were not just helpless victims of this process (though in the long term they were indeed victims); they were also opportunists, taking advantage of new possibilities. The Comanches, for example, thrived by becoming a supreme horse culture; they turned the tables on the Spaniards and kept them sidelined on the peripheries of the southern Great Plains until Spain's overextended empire collapsed and Mexico took over in 1821.

The French approached the Great Plains from two directions: from Montreal and the Great Lakes into what is now lower Manitoba, and from the lower Mississippi River valley via the Red and Arkansas Rivers into the southern grasslands (fig. 4). In the north, French fur traders established a presence in 1738 when they built Fort La Reine on the north bank of the Assiniboine River in present-day Manitoba. Unlike the Spaniards, the French did not remain on the margins of the Great Plains but instead incorporated themselves into Indian societies through trade and marriage, so producing the Métis, an ethnicity of mixed Indian and French heritage that is now recognized in the Canadian Constitution as an Aboriginal People.

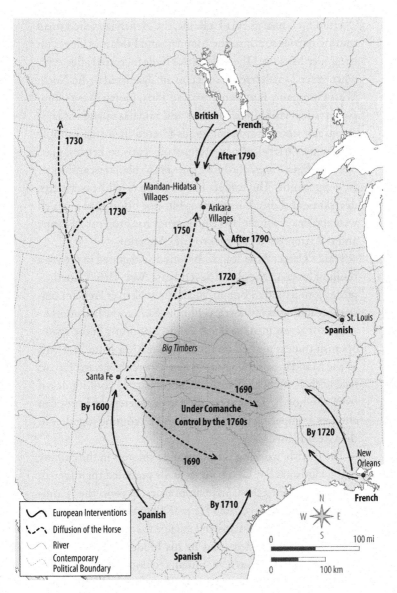

British **French**

After 1790

1730

1730

Mandan-Hidatsa
Villages

Arikara
Villages

1750

After 1790

1720

St. Louis

Spanish

Big Timbers

Santa Fe

1690

By 1600

**Under Comanche
Control by the 1760s**

By 1720

New
Orleans

1690

French

1690

By 1710

Spanish

Spanish

N
W   E
S

0   100 mi

0   100 km

Legend	
ᔑ	European Interventions
ᔑ	Diffusion of the Horse
ᔑ	River
	Contemporary Political Boundary

4. Early geographies. Created by Ezra J. Zeitler.

From their base at Fort La Reine, the French launched small trading parties south to the Mandan and Hidatsa villages on the upper Missouri. The scale of this trade increased after 1770, when several small trading concerns amalgamated as the North West Company. Between 1770 and 1803, North West Company traders visited the Mandan and Hidatsa villages at least seventeen times. European goods filtered in, a small supply (but wide variety) of new items from guns to kettles, glass beads to brass rings, corduroy trousers to blankets, and sugar to peppermint. The traders in return received beaver pelts, deerskins, and dried bison meat but not bison robes, which were too heavy for the overland journey back to Fort La Reine and the attenuated portages to Lake Superior.

France's larger American ambitions disintegrated in 1763 as a result of losses in the global Seven Years' War. Their Canadian possessions passed to Britain, and Spain took over French Louisiana, reaching as far north as Illinois. Spain now had another avenue of access into the Great Plains. Beginning in the 1790s, Spanish traders pushed up the Missouri River from St. Louis to the Mandan and Hidatsa villages, where they came face to face with French and British trading parties coming down from the north. These were the far perimeters of European empires, competing for the world, and all coming together in the Great Plains.

The British, working as traders and explorers in the employ of the Hudson's Bay Company, actually preceded their French counterparts into the Canadian prairies. In 1690 the "Company" sent nineteen-year-old Henry Kelsay west from Hudson's Bay to contact the Indians and engage them in the fur trade. Kelsay—a boy characterized by his Hudson's Bay employers as "delighting much in Indians' company"—may have reached the Rocky Mountains and lived with the Blackfeet for a while. But the British did not follow up, preferring to have the Indians bring their furs to the trading posts on Hudson's Bay.

This all changed after 1770. The Hudson's Bay Company went into direct competition with the North West Company, building posts in the Assiniboine and Red River valleys and dispatching trading parties to the Mandans and Hidatsas. The rivalry between the two companies simmered until 1821, when the Hudson's Bay Company absorbed its French competitors. French fur traders, however, continued to be the rank and file of the fur business on the northern Great Plains, even after American fur companies took control in the 1820s.

In 1803, at the time of the transfer of Louisiana from France to the United States, Europeans amounted to only a handful of strangers on the Great Plains, plying their trade and political ambitions among powerful Indian nations like the Comanches (who may have numbered forty thousand by the 1770s). The impact of these few, however, was immense, bringing short-term benefits to the Indians but also long-term catastrophe. The three main impacts were horses, guns, and disease, especially smallpox.

The introduction of the horse (or rather, reintroduction, because horses had been one of the casualties of the Pleistocene die-off) from Spain's New Mexico colony in 1650 transformed the world of the pedestrian hunters. The Spaniards actually prohibited trade in horses (and guns), not wanting mounted Indian warriors on their doorstep. But horses were surreptitiously traded by the Pueblo Indians, and by the 1650s nearby Apaches were making full use of this new asset. After the Pueblo revolt of 1680 (which threw off Spanish control for twelve years), large numbers of horses were taken, or traded, by the Indians of the southern Great Plains. Horses proliferated there in a physical setting that was not so different from their places of origin, North Africa and the arid interior of Spain.

The lure of horses and a liberated life as mounted bison hunters pulled Indians south toward the source. By 1710 the Comanches had migrated from the northern Great Plains via the central Rockies onto the horse-rich grasslands of the southern plains. Within a generation they were a fully mounted society. They drove the Apaches to the fringes of the region and established a trading and raiding empire that stretched from the Arkansas River to the Rio Grande (fig. 4). Similarly, in the second half of the eighteenth century, the Kiowas moved from the Black Hills to the southern Great Plains, where they made a necessary accommodation with the Comanches and fully engaged in the horse trade. Soon after, several bands of the Cheyennes and Arapahos relocated from the Black Hills to the upper Arkansas valley. There they became middlemen, acquiring horses from the Comanches and funneling them to the Indians of the northern Plains.

Horses reached the Pawnees in the central Great Plains by 1720 and the Crows and Blackfeet in the northern Great Plains by 1740 (fig. 4). The diffusion wave took about a century to wash over the entire region. But horses remained a scarce resource in the region's northern reaches, because most perished in the severe winters. Whereas an average Comanche family in 1800 owned thirty-five horses, a Blackfeet family was fortunate to have one or two. In fact, many Blackfeet families had no horses at all, and dogs remained the primary beast of burden.

The attraction of the horse was irresistible. Distance was overcome, mounted Indians could travel farther to locate bison herds or water, and they could trade and raid widely. Women no longer had to carry heavy loads. Many more bison could be killed by equestrian hunters armed with bows and arrows than by using traditional driving and pounding methods (though these continued among horse-poor Indians). Horses also allowed farming Indians like the Omahas and Pawnees to travel greater distances to the western bison ranges, and to carry larger loads of meat and robes back to their villages. Conceivably, had they been given the time, the farming Indians might have made a full-blown transition to the hunting life, just as the Crows and Cheyennes did in the late eighteenth century. But their agriculturally based religious ceremonies, which, in their minds, secured the annual cycle of life, would have made this difficult.

The arrival of horses, however, also set in motion a series of changes that would prove destabilizing and even disastrous for the Indians. Horses needed constant care, especially the daily provision of forage and water. The same horses that had allowed the Comanches to rise to power were a real challenge to maintain. The Indians were obliged to move their settlements every few days because their horses left the surrounding grasslands grazed to the ground. In fact, the Comanches became horse herders, practicing pastoralism, as much as bison hunters.

Farming Indians like the Pawnees found it impossible to sustain thousands of horses at their villages year-round. So their long bison hunts on the western High Plains became a matter not only of securing robes and meat but also of keeping their horses alive. Eventually, in the nineteenth century, the competition between horses and bison for grass and water would be instrumental in the decline of the bison herds and in the associated loss of Indian independence.

Horses revolutionized the practice of warfare on the Great Plains. Before the horse, there were armed conflicts over favored places, or for revenge, or as a result of simple enmity. But there was little reason for the Indians to raid each other. There wasn't much to plunder. All the Indians had supplies of dogs, clothing, bows, dried meat, and stone tools and weapons. There was also the buffer of raw space between them. It made little sense to make long journeys to obtain what was already at hand.

Besides, without horses, there was no way to quickly carry large amounts of stolen items back to the home encampment.

Horses changed all this. They broke through the buffer of distance and introduced the new possibility of amassing property. They became both the cause and the objective of war. A young man, marking out a position for himself in the world, could never have too many horses. They could be used as currency to acquire desirable wives, or an empowering gun, or to give as gifts to others, so earning a reputation for generosity, which was a prerequisite for respect and status. As Lone Chief, the son of a deceased Pawnee chief, was told by his mother: "It is not the man who stays in the lodge that becomes great; it is the man who works, who sweats, who is always tired from going on the warpath."

Whereas self-propagating horses gave the Indians independence, widening the horizons of their lives, guns created a dependency on the European traders because there was always a need for more, and also for ammunition and powder. Guns—even the primitive, muzzle-loading flintlocks of the time—quickly became indispensable in war because of their penetrative power and deadly impact from a distance. In the late eighteenth century, guns became essential for survival. For example, the Spanish trader Jean Baptiste Truteau, who led an exploring expedition to the upper Missouri in 1794, described how guns and ammunition were a necessity to the Arikaras because they protected them from "formidable enemies who so often carry off their children."

Before 1800 nearly all the guns imported into the Great Plains came from French or British traders, or from intermediaries like the Crees and Assiniboines, who acquired them at an early date and passed them on at a profit. On the northern Great Plains, the southerly and westerly spread of the gun frontier met the northeasterly movement of the horse frontier at the

Missouri River around 1750. Whereas there had been some degree of equality among the various Indian groups in the past, now there were discrepancies of power: some Indians had horses but not guns, some had guns but not horses, and some had the great advantage of having both. How these inequalities played out in warfare was related in vivid detail by an old Cree Indian, Saukamappee, to the British trader and explorer David Thompson in the winter of 1786–87. Saukamappee's story runs like a thread through the momentous events of the eighteenth century.

Around 1730, when Saukamappee was still a teenager, he joined his father in a party of twenty Cree warriors and traveled west to assist the Piegan Blackfeet in a war with the Shoshonis (Snakes), who were asserting their authority on the northwestern plains. The Crees had a few guns and a little ammunition, but they had left these at home with their families for hunting and protection. They carried lances, a few with metal points, bows and arrows (again, some with metal points), and stone axes. Saukamappee also had an iron knife of which he was particularly proud.

After joining the Piegans, and a few days of speeches and feasting, they prepared to engage the enemy. Saukamappee estimated that they amounted to 350 warriors, a powerful infantry force, but fewer than the Shoshonis. The combatants faced off against each other in long lines, crouching behind their hide shields. Saukamappee was alarmed to find that the Shoshonis had better bows: they had wrapped bison sinews around the wood, "which made them very elastic," and their arrows flew all around. But the arrows were only tipped with flint, and they broke when they struck the shields. Even the Crees' metal-tipped arrows just hung harmlessly in the shields. Consequently, from this large-scale encounter, only a few Indians were wounded, no one was killed, and not a single scalp was taken. Saukamappee told Thompson that this was generally the result in evenly pitched battles before the adoption of the horse and gun.

About ten years later, Saukamappee continued, he again joined the Piegans to fight the Shoshonis, this time with a war party of ten Crees and Assiniboines. He was now married and had not wanted to go, but his wife's family had asked him to take a Shoshoni scalp and bring it back for inclusion in their medicine bundle. Saukamappee explained to Thompson that since the last encounter, "the affairs of both parties had changed." His war party had guns and was considered by their Piegan allies (who did not yet have guns) to be the "strength of the battle." But they knew that the Shoshonis had horses (*misstutim* or "big dogs"), because in a previous battle with the on-foot Piegans they had charged, "swift as the deer," and chopped down many with their stone axes.

Saukamappee's allied force soon encountered a large Shoshoni war party that was on foot, probably because their horses were still few. They lined up in typical formation, hiding behind their shields, periodically stepping out to fire their arrows. Saukamappee and his men kept their guns hidden until the lines were sixty yards apart. Then they opened fire, causing "consternation and dismay along their whole line." Many Shoshonis were killed, and competition for their scalps was so fierce that Saukamappee was initially unable to secure one for his wife's family. The next day the Piegan War Chief gave a scalp to each member of Saukamappee's party in recognition of the decisive role they had played in the battle.

Clearly, with the advent of the horse and gun, warfare was more deadly, and the Great Plains had become an increasingly perilous place. The American explorers Meriwether Lewis and William Clark, ascending the Missouri River in 1804, had been asked to ascertain for each tribe they encountered "the names of the nations with whom they are at war." More often than not, they recorded "with all nations generally," or words to that effect. By that time, on the Great Plains, the warpath led in every direction.

The danger was intensified by the migration of the Sioux (Yanktons, Yanktonais, and especially the seven divisions of the Tetons) from the upper Midwest, across the Missouri River by 1800, and on relentlessly to the Black Hills. They were pushed from the Midwest by the decline of the fur trade—caused by the depletion of beaver populations—and pulled to the Great Plains by the attraction of the bison herds and easier access to horses. Bison robes soon became the main product of the Great Plains fur trade because the Missouri River route to St. Louis made the transportation of such bulky items possible. Armed with guns, initially from French traders and later from Americans, and increasingly mounted, the imperial force of the Sioux swept all before them, pushing the Crows to the north and west and the Kiowas to the south, and entering into a long-lasting alliance with the Cheyennes and Arapahos. Whereas previously there had been neutral zones, wide spaces between Indian homelands, now all the hunting range was contested. The Sioux also dominated the village Indians along the Missouri River, from the Omahas in present-day Nebraska north to the Mandans and Hidatsas. By 1800 the latter two tribes were under perpetual siege, hiding in their heavily fortified villages, unable to venture out to hunt because of the imminent threat of Sioux.

The westward surge of the Sioux was aided and abetted by smallpox, the third and most damaging of the European introductions. Indians and Europeans alike were stricken by this virulent virus, but its effect was less deadly for the Europeans because they had developed a degree of immunity after centuries of exposure to this Old World disease. Indians had no such immunity, at least not until they had contracted, then survived, an infection. So this set in motion the tragedy of repeating catastrophes wherein Indians lost large segments of their populations (mortality rates of 50 percent or more were common, all within a few weeks), including generations of children who had not lived through a previous epidemic and therefore had no immunity.

Smallpox spread mainly through human contact via the respiratory tract and, after a brief incubation period, progressed rapidly and painfully until the afflicted person was covered with suppurating lesions, both on the inside and the outside of the body. Vibrant settlements were turned overnight into open graveyards where bodies lay rotting on the ground. The disease was especially calamitous in the crowded villages of the farming Indians, while more decentralized societies like the Sioux tended to be affected less, and this swung the balance of power in their favor. The Arikaras, for example, were reduced from thirty-two villages to just two, and from four thousand warriors to five hundred, by three smallpox epidemics in the second half of the eighteenth century. When Lewis and Clark passed by their remnant villages in 1804, they recorded that the decimated Arikaras were living as "tenants at will" to the Sioux.

Not that the Sioux were unaffected by smallpox. In fact, the terrible epidemic that swept over the Great Plains from 1779 to 1783, taking out two-thirds of the eastern Comanches and reducing the Crows from two thousand to three hundred lodges, also devastated the Sioux. Their winter counts—pictorial histories of the major events of each year—for 1779–80 and 1780–81 were called, respectively, the "Smallpox-used-them-up winter" and the "Smallpox-used-them-up-again winter." They depicted an afflicted person, twisted with pain, and the 1779–80 count also showed the symbol for cramped bowels (fig. 5). The winter count for 1801–2 showed a recurrence of smallpox,

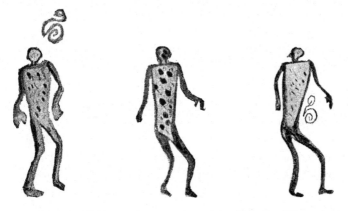

5. Baptiste Good's Winter Counts: 1779–80, Smallpox-Used-Them-Up Winter; 1780–81, Smallpox-Used-Them-Up-Again Winter; 1801–2, Smallpox-Used-Them-Up-Again Winter. Mallery, *Picture-Writing of the American Indians*, 308, 313.

but it is possible that the Sioux, like the Crees to the north, had acquired a degree of immunity from early and repeated contact with traders (and therefore with smallpox), so their population began an upward trajectory in the early nineteenth century, while the numbers of the village Indians continued to plummet.

Saukamappee was an eyewitness to the brutal effects of smallpox in 1781, though he had no idea what he was witnessing. He and his fellow Piegans (he had joined them permanently by this time) set out to raid a Shoshoni camp in the Red Deer River valley. They quickly realized that something was wrong: there was no sign of human activity in the camp, and bison were grazing right up to the tipis. Still, they attacked, cutting through the covers of the tipis and preparing to fight. Then, as Saukamappee told David Thompson, "our war whoops instantly stopt, our eyes were appalled with terror; there was no one to fight with but the dead and dying, each a mass of corruption." Badly shaken, Saukamappee and his men withdrew, concluding that "the Bad Spirit had made himself master of the camp and destroyed them."

The "Bad Spirit" then joined Saukamappee's party, and within a few days smallpox was raging among the Piegans. "We had no belief," Saukamappee said, "that one Man could give it to another, any more than a wounded Man could give his wound to another." Altogether, about half of the Piegans died. Saukamappee described how "tears, shrieks, and howlings of despair" filled their camps; war was no longer possible, just survival. "Our hearts were low and dejected," Saukamappee said, and he realized then that the Piegans would "never be the same people again." The smallpox epidemics continued through the first half of the nineteenth century, landing on the Indians like breakers on a beach, until American inoculation efforts and acquired immunity mitigated the terrible effects.

This was the maelstrom of a world that the United States inherited in 1803. It was a world largely unknown to them. The maps of the day show the Great Plains as a void, or a fiction of imaginary geographies. But the Great Plains was anything but a void to the Indians. It was filled with intimately known homelands and traditional ways of life that had gone on since time immemorial, but which now were in flux because of the arrival of strangers who had come to stay forever.

CHAPTER TWO

Land and Life around 1803

Despite the drastic effects of European contact—the rapid transition from the Stone Age to the Iron Age, the dreadful depleting epidemics, the intensified warfare—Plains Indian life at the beginning of the nineteenth century still followed the age-old cycles. This was the Indians' stability in an increasingly unstable world. The farming Indians of the eastern Great Plains continued to divide their year between cultivating crops at their villages and hunting bison on the western range, spreading their subsistence base across the entire breadth of the region; the western hunters still calibrated their movements to the bison herds, living in small family bands for much of the year, and gathering in large camps in summer for communal hunts, feasting, trading, and celebration of life. And while there was considerable religious diversity among the different nations of Plains Indians, they all believed (as they probably always had) in the great unifying power of the life force, which they saw manifested all around them, in the movements of the heavens, the behavior of animals, the messages of dreams, and the reliable order of day and night, winter and summer.

The Plains Indians were able to continue living in traditional ways (albeit under escalating stress) because their new sovereign, the United States, did not yet covet their lands. The purchase of Louisiana from France in 1803, encompassing all of the American Great Plains north of the Red and Arkansas Rivers, served two immediate purposes for the United States: first, the vast area would be used as a depository for eastern Indians who were blocking the restless American advance across the Appalachians and on to the Mississippi River; and second, this concentration of Indians, both resident and introduced, in the Great Plains would in turn prevent settlers from spreading *too* far west and threatening the cohesion of the new nation. Only licensed traders would be allowed into "Indian Country" (this is how it was labeled on maps of the time), and they of course wanted the Indians to keep living traditionally because it was through Indian labor that they got their furs and profits. So the Plains Indians were given a brief respite, until their lands too were needed by the United States, and then they were quickly taken from them.

Territories

The American plans for the Great Plains as an Indian consolidation zone and a barrier containing frontier expansion were explicit in President Thomas Jefferson's instructions to his explorers, Meriwether Lewis and William Clark. In addition to finding the long-sought-after route to the Pacific (and beyond to the Indies) and informing the Indians that they now had a new "Great Father," Lewis and Clark were charged with identifying "the boundaries of the Country which they claim," as a prerequisite for moving in displaced Indians from east of the Mississippi.

So it was wishful thinking, perhaps, and certainly geopolitically convenient, that Lewis and Clark concluded that most of the Plains Indian nations had "no idea of an exclusive possession of any country." This being the case, Lewis and Clark believed that they "would not object to the introduction of any well disposed Indians" from the east.

More likely, Lewis and Clark were simply blinded by their own Euro-American conception of territories as distinct pieces of land that were owned, individually and nationally, and which had boundaries that were defined, demarcated, and defended. They couldn't be expected to understand that all Plains Indians claimed territories—homelands—that they considered their own, and which contained their histories, expressed their religions, and gave them subsistence. To the Indians, territoriality was synonymous with occupancy: their territories were where they lived over the course of the year, and year after year. They were deeply committed to place.

The Otoes, for example, one of the nations described by Lewis and Clark as claiming no territory, had inhabited villages on the lower Platte River, near its junction with the Missouri, for a century by the time the explorers passed by. Their homeland was what is now southeastern Nebraska, and their commitment to the land ran deep. Even the names of their months expressed this geographical connection: February was "the month of the water frog," and October was "the mating of the deer." When the Otoes were squeezed out of their homeland in 1876 and 1881, and moved south to Indian Territory (later Oklahoma), their names for the months lost their significance, their stories (histories) lost their context, and their religion lost its reference points.

A map of Indian territories at the beginning of the nineteenth century (fig.6) gives a general idea of the geographical distribution of the various Plains Indian nations, from the Blackfeet and Assiniboines in the north to the Comanches and Wichitas at the south. The map distorts through simplification: those authoritative-looking boundary lines between territories were really transition zones. Moreover, in 1803, these territories were in flux, expanding and contracting with the changing fortunes of each people. For example, Lewis and Clark described how the Missourias had recently been compelled by "repeated attacks of the smallpox together with their war with the Saukies (Sauk) and Renars (Fox)" to abandon their homeland in Missouri and seek sanctuary with their relatives, the Otoes. Similarly, smallpox and attacks by the Sioux had forced the Mandans to vacate their communal hunting grounds between the Missouri and Little Missouri Rivers and retreat into their stockaded villages.

On the other hand, the Comanches and Sioux, by taking advantage of new hunting, trading, and raiding opportunities and mastering the art of mounted warfare, constantly expanded their territorial control during the first half of the nineteenth century at the expense of neighboring groups. The Cheyennes, described by Lewis and Clark as a "remnant of a nation once respectable in numbers" were one of these dispossessed peoples. They had formerly occupied a village on the Missouri and raised crops. But, as Lewis and Clark explained, "being oppressed by the Sioux . . . they fled to the Black Hills" and "wander in the quest of the buffaloe, having no fixed residence."

Structurally and functionally, the traditional Indian territories might be considered as gradations from a core. This construction is particularly applicable to the territories of the village Indians. Their core areas contained their villages, agricultural lands, and most important sacred sites. Each core was discrete, separate from those of other Indians, although after the acquisition of the horse, and the resulting compression of space, they were vulnerable to enemy raids. Beyond each core was a domain of overlapping and contested hunting ranges. And beyond the domain was a far-flung sphere of trading and raiding that reached right into the core areas of other Indians.

The core area of the Pawnees, for example, lay in the fertile, wooded valleys of the Platte and Loup Rivers in central Nebraska. Their roots were deep in this place, reaching back

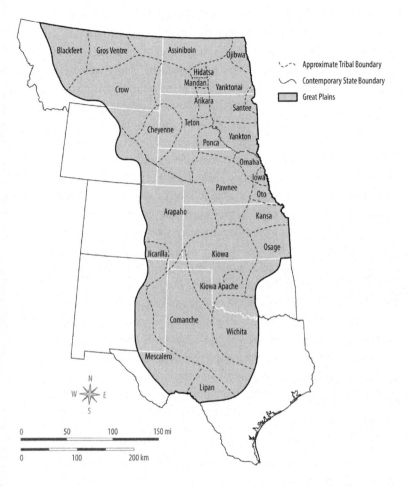

Legend:
- Approximate Tribal Boundary
- Contemporary State Boundary
- Great Plains

Blackfeet, Gros Ventre, Assiniboin, Ojibwa, Crow, Hidatsa, Mandan, Yanktonai, Arikara, Santee, Cheyenne, Teton, Yankton, Ponca, Omaha, Iowa, Pawnee, Oto, Arapaho, Kansa, Jicarilla, Kiowa, Osage, Kiowa Apache, Comanche, Wichita, Mescalero, Lipan

0 50 100 150 mi
0 100 200 km

6. American Indian territories on the Great Plains, 1803. Created by Ezra J. Zeitler.

hundreds of years. Each of the four bands of the Pawnee Confederation had its own village, or villages, in this core area. The villages were situated on the river terraces, with their fertile alluvial soils and water and timber nearby. These were large, fortified settlements, some with as many as two hundred earth lodges, housing more than three thousand people. There were more people in a single Pawnee village in 1803 than in St. Louis, the largest western town. Outside the villages, a humanized landscape of agricultural fields and deforested ground extended for miles along the valleys. The villages were moved every few years as the local supplies of wood were depleted. Graveyards, where the spirits of ancestors were believed to live, lay on the bluffs surrounding the villages, yet another attachment to their homeland.

Almost all of the Pawnees' animal lodges were located in their homeland. Pawnees, seeking insights and the power to heal, went to these sacred sites to fast and dream. The animals—Pawnees considered all animals to be sacred—were seen as intermediaries between the celestial gods (sun, moon, and stars) and humans. They occupied underground lodges, situated mainly where hills and rivers came together. The most powerful animal lodge was Pa:haku ("mound on the water"), located at the base of high wooded bluffs rising above the Platte. Pawnees who received the gift of visions from the animals became doctors in their society, practicing Medicine Lodge ceremonies that drew on the power of these animals to assure good fortune in life. Pawnee religion, like the religions of all Plains Indians, was tied to place, and it lost much of its meaning when the sacred sites passed into the hands of others.

The Pawnees' hunting domain stretched mainly west and southwest from the village core. Lewis and Clark reported that the Pawnees hunted "high up on the Plat" and at the headwaters of the Kansas River. They claimed this bison range as their own, but the Kansas Indians, one of the many enemies of the Pawnees, also claimed it, and so did the Cheyennes and, over time, the Sioux. As the nineteenth century progressed, and the bison herds diminished, these overlapping domains became increasingly disputed zones of conflict, rather than places of sanctuary.

The peripheries of the Pawnee world, where they traded and raided, reached from the upper Missouri to the Spanish settlements in New Mexico. They traded with their Caddoan-speaking relatives, the Arikaras to the north and the Wichitas to the south, and they alternately traded with and raided the Spaniards, and later the Mexicans, for horses. By the 1820s the Pawnees were regularly raiding the Santa Fe Trail between Missouri and New Mexico, and beyond, deep into the Rio Grande country. Mexican authorities were so outraged that they threatened to declare war on the Pawnees if the United States did not restrain them.

Beyond even this wide orbit of trading and raiding there was the outward reach of exploration, the human desire to know what lay over the horizon. In 1806, for example, when the American explorer Zebulon Pike was making his way to the Pawnee villages, he was accompanied by two young Pawnees who were returning, they claimed, from a visit to Washington DC to meet the president. When they reached the villages, the Pawnee explorers were ridiculed as liars and punished for undertaking an unsanctioned journey. But the fact that they had in their possession medals with President Jefferson's image on them, and documents bearing the president's signature, suggests that there was truth to their extraordinary claim. More locally, Indians frequently visited St. Louis; Big Elk, chief of the Omahas, had been there five times by 1813. Plains Indians were exploring Americans, just as much as the other way around.

The territories of the bison hunters were less obvious gradations from a core: as Lewis and Clark recognized, they simply "claim the country in which they rove." But these hunting territories were also filled with sacred meaning and treasured places. Many physical features in Blackfeet country, for example, were associated with Old Man, their creator. At one such place, Old Man, denied a bride, had turned himself into a pine tree, which was a site of Blackfeet pilgrimage for many years. Bear Butte, at the northern edge of the Black Hills was (and is) a venerated holy site to both the Cheyennes and Sioux. Other places of sacred significance, all connections to a homeland, were where famous victories had been achieved, or where loved ones had been lost, or visions received. It wasn't time that mattered (because time repeated every year), but place, where history, religion, and life converged.

This intimate attachment to a home territory was methodically explained by the Crow chief Arapooish to the trapper Robert Campbell, sometime in the 1820s. Arapooish started by saying, "The Crow country is a good country; the Great Spirit put it in exactly the right place; while you are in it you fare well; whenever you go out of it, whichever way you travel, you fare worse." If you go to the south, Arapooish elaborated, the land is barren, the water is bad, and "fever and ague abound"; to the north it is too cold to keep horses and you are, therefore, obliged to "travel with dogs"; to the west, on the Columbia, the Indians are reduced to eating fish, "a poor food" in Arapooish's opinion; and to the east you have to drink the muddy waters of the Missouri, which even the Crow's dogs would disdain. Arapooish finished his eulogy to home by repeating his main message: "the Crow country is in exactly the right place. Everything good is found there. There is no country like the Crow country."

In 1803 all the homelands of the Plains Indians were under pressure, ultimately because of the European and American presence in North America, which had sent shock waves through the region and transformed it into a disease-drenched war zone. But none of these homelands had yet been bought or taken. That inexorable process would begin in 1818, when the Quapaws sold what is now southern Oklahoma to make room for displaced Indians from the southeastern United States. The process of dispossession would escalate over the course of the nineteenth century, until the Plains Indians were left with only fragments of the homelands they had cherished, if indeed they retained any at all. But for a few decades in the early 1800s this was still completely "Indian Country," and the rhythms of life from spring to spring went on as before.

Annual Cycles

Each Plains Indian society had, in detail, its own annual cycle, because each occupied its own ecological niche, with specific resources and significant places. For example, the Comanches, lords of the southern Plains, had no fixed settlements for most of the year but instead moved their camps every few days in an unceasing search for pasture and water for their innumerable horses. In late November, following a large fall bison hunt (which all the Great Plains bison hunters undertook), the Comanches amassed in large winter camps along the upper Arkansas River or the Canadian, Red, Brazos, and Colorado Rivers, forming bustling settlements that extended for miles and which attracted foreign traders who sought their horses, mules, meat, and slaves. This was a different regime from that of the bison hunters of the northern Plains, who scattered in small bands in the harsh winters to secluded valleys, allocating themselves out to the scarce resources. Still, despite the diversity and complexity of Indian life on the Great Plains, a distinction can be drawn between the annual cycle of the bison hunters and that of the village Indians, who were fixed in place by their farming activities for a portion of the year.

The Blackfeet, typical enough of the bison hunters of the northern Plains, emerged from their dispersed winter camps in spring, as the geese flew north. Their year officially began with the Medicine Pipe ceremony, held after the first thunderstorm of the season. The sacred bundles, containing ornately decorated pipe stems (believed to be a gift from the all-powerful sun) as well as other holy objects, were opened and their power to heal and protect renewed. At the same time, the bison herds that the Blackfeet relied on for the fundamentals of life were also leaving their winter quarters in the wooded valleys and moving out onto the greening plains. They separated into small groups of mature bulls and larger companies of cows, calves, and yearlings, circulating around a home range, seeking grass and water.

Spring was also the main season for Blackfeet women (and for Indian women throughout the Great Plains) to gather *pomme blanche* (prairie potatoes, or turnips), a starchy root that grew on the dry prairie in the full sun. This root was most easily collected in spring and early summer, when it flowered, because when the plant ripened the stems fell off, and it became hard to find. The roots were eaten fresh, either cooked or uncooked, or else dried for winter use when food was sometimes in short supply. With great ceremony, Blackfeet men planted Indian tobacco (the Blackfeet's only agricultural endeavor) in beds that the women and children had cleared and manured with elk and deer droppings. Geese and duck eggs, a seasonal boon, were collected too, though the birds themselves were not much used for food, their procurement being more trouble than the meat was worth in a place where bison abounded.

In summer the female bison came into heat and the bull and calf divisions coalesced into massive herds for the rut.

7. *Encampment of the Piekann Indians*, 1833. Karl Bodmer (Swiss, 1809–93), Charles Beyer and Johann Hürlimann, engravers, aquatint, etching, and stipple, hand-colored on paper. Courtesy of the Joslyn Art Museum, Omaha, Nebraska, Gift of the Enron Art Foundation.

The Blackfeet bands now came together for large communal hunts that provided meat and hides, which were tanned on both sides (the hair of the robes being thin in summer) for use as tipi covers, moccasins, and leggings (fig. 7). Camus roots, which grew abundantly in wet meadows on the east side of the Rockies, were dug up, cooked in large pits, and eaten like roasted chestnuts or dried in the sun and stored. Purple sarvis berries (serviceberries) were picked and eaten fresh, used to flavor soups, or dried and pounded and, with other dried fruits, added to the cured bison meat to provide a nutritious pemmican for the lean months.

In August on the first full moon after the sarvis berries ripened, all the bands came together for the Medicine Lodge ceremony, the Blackfeet version of the Sun Dance. This grand midsummer festival varied greatly from one Plains Indian group to another, with each having its own songs, dances, and prayers. Among the Blackfeet, it was generally a woman who made the vow to sponsor the Medicine Lodge, perhaps to ensure the safety of a husband who was away raiding, to heal a child who was sick, or simply to sacrifice for the general good of the people. The Medicine Lodge woman would dry hundreds of bison tongues for use in the ceremonies, while young men built a circular lodge with a large center pole and a door facing east toward the rising sun. The Medicine Lodge woman, her face and hands covered with red paint, fasted for four days inside her tipi. Then, when everything had been prepared, she walked, head bowed, to the Medicine Lodge, where she cut up the tongues and gave a small piece to every man, woman, and child. Each held up the offering to the sun, praying for the assistance of this supreme power in assuring spiritual and material welfare for the Blackfeet.

The Medicine Lodge was a communal ceremony in which everyone participated. It solidified tribal identity for a people who lived apart for most of the year. It was also the occasion for warrior societies and other religious organizations to perform their dances and rituals, including rituals of mortification where young men were suspended from the center post, skewered through their breasts, fulfilling vows they had made the previous year, in gratitude perhaps for surviving war or sickness. On the fourth day, after everyone had dedicated his or her presents to the all-powerful sun, and all the tongues had been consumed, the ceremony ended. As a result of the sacrifices of the Medicine Lodge woman, and all the associated dances, mortifications, and prayers, the fortunes of the Blackfeet were now in the hands of providence, and assured.

In fall the Blackfeet separated again into family bands to hunt bison on the grasslands. Sometimes they came together in camps near buffalo jumps and pounds, because even after the adoption of horses, these ancient methods of procurement persisted. The fall bison hunt was vital for winter subsistence. The bison robes were now thick, so they were tanned only on one side and used for winter warmth. The meat, taken from cows and calves (the meat of the old bulls was tough), was dried, mixed with wild plums and other fruits, and stored in bison hide bags. The tobacco crop was harvested and, after the singing of songs to the sun, dried for use over the course of the year in the smoke offerings that were part of every ceremony, and part of everyday life.

In November, as the snow accumulated, the bands of the Blackfeet went into dispersed winter camps in river valleys where the bison also gathered and where there was water, grass for horses, and wood for fuel. Cottonwood bark and new branches were collected as an effective supplementary forage for horses. Among the favored winter grounds for the Blackfeet were the Porcupine Hills, the Milk and Marias River valleys, the junction of the Belly and Saint Mary Rivers in southwestern Alberta, and the headwaters of the Missouri, where the Great Plains and Rocky Mountains come together. Sometimes they would stay in a single camp all winter; more often they would make short moves as the local fuel and forage were exhausted. The owners of the beaver bundle kept a count of the passage of the season with sticks, and anticipated the time when the geese would fly north and the year would begin again with the consecration of the Medicine Pipe bundles.

The Pawnees, village Indians of central Nebraska, also began their year with the signal of the first thunder. Specifically for the Skiri Pawnee (there was much ceremonial difference even *within* the Pawnee confederation), the signal was the first thunder after the appearance of two small twinkling stars (the Swimming Ducks) in the northeastern sky, near the Milky Way. The thunder announced the renewal of life after the dead of winter, and dramatic ceremonies each spring recalled the original creation of the world. In the first week of May, as the willows turned green and after the planting ceremonies had been performed, the Pawnee women began to prepare the ground for crops.

The fields, each about an acre or two in size, were allocated by the chiefs of each Pawnee village. Unlike the Blackfeet and other bison hunters, the village Indians were stratified societies, with hereditary leadership and social layers, from chiefs, priests, and doctors down to commoners. Families with high status received the more convenient and safer plots close to the village. The old vegetation was burned, adding potash to the already fertile alluvial soil of the river terrace, which the women hoed into mounds using a bison shoulder blade (scapula) attached to a wooden handle. Corn was planted first, five to seven kernels in each mound. Beans were planted alongside the corn, and as they grew they used the corn stalks for support. Then pumpkins, squash, and watermelons were cultivated between the mounds, providing a buffer that preserved the integrity of the Pawnee's ten pure varieties of corn. Sunflowers were sometimes sown around the perimeters of the fields, forming a living fence that denoted the women's ownership of the plot for the duration of the agricultural season. Tobacco was planted separately by the men on a patch of ground where dried grass had been piled and burned. The fact that corn, and corn alone, was the focus of the Pawnee's planting and creation ceremonies indicates its prime position in Pawnee life, although by 1803, thanks to horses and bulk transportation, about half of the food supply came from bison.

At the beginning of June, when the corn was about three feet high, the mounds were hoed and weeded a final time, and the Pawnees began their preparations for the summer bison hunt, which would last until September. All the Pawnees participated in the hunt, except for a few "stay-at-homes" who were too old or sick to travel, or who, for reasons of their own, had decided not to go.

The practical preparations for the hunt involved the men making bows strung with bison sinew and arranging for specialized arrow makers to furnish them each with about thirty arrows. Women would sew tipi covers and pack their stocks of dried corn, beans, and pemmican in hide parfleches. The earth lodges were cleaned and closed; sometimes sticks were latticed across the doorway, so that any intrusion would be apparent. Preparations completed, the Pawnees turned to the southwest and began their journey to the bison range, leaving their crops to ripen unattended in the heat of the Nebraska summer sun.

The procession of the four bands, each led by a chief, to the hunting grounds was slow and methodical. Ten miles a day was good progress, considering that it took about three hours to set up camp each evening and again to break camp in the morning. All together, it was about a twenty-day trek. If anything, the women's workload was even heavier on the hunt than at the villages and included cooking, cleaning, and carrying as well as taking care of the tipis and the sacred bundles.

The Pawnees traced the creeks and rivers down to the valleys of the Solomon and Republican Rivers, where they expected to encounter the bison herds. At each stage of the hunt there were ceremonies to ensure success: to prevent rain, for example, because rain caused the bowstrings to slacken, the tanned hides to harden, and the dried meat to rot. The actual hunts were strictly regulated, and anyone who attacked without permission was punished. Like all Plains Indians, the Pawnees used the summer hides, tanned on both sides by the women, for clothes and tipi covers. The choice parts of the meat were eaten fresh in religious feasts or dried for use over the course of the year. In late August, when the prairie goldenrod bloomed on the western plains and the south star, Canopus, appeared in the sky, the Pawnees knew that it was time to return home for the harvest. The journey home was slower than the migration out to the range because now their horses were carrying heavy loads of hides and meat.

Back at the villages, some of the corn (by this time towering eight feet high over the prairie) was picked green and eaten fresh after the ears had been roasted on a fire. The bean, pumpkin, squash, and watermelon harvests followed, and, finally, in October, the mature corn was picked. This was an important food collecting season too. *Pomme blanche* grew so abundantly in the sandy soils along the Loup fork of the Platte River that it was called, in translation, the "Potato River." Ground beans were also gathered, sometimes from caches that had already been made by prairie voles; the Pawnee women were careful to leave a few kernels of corn in exchange. Fall generally was a season of plenty and great activity, with crops being brought in from the fields, corn roasting on fires and drying on scaffolds, women sitting in circles scraping kernels from the ears using clamshells, and digging the cache pits where the dried food was stored in hide sacks until November, when the Pawnee's attention again turned to the bison range.

By late summer, the prairie grasses around the villages had dried up and lost their nutritional value. The Pawnees sent their horses (they had about eight thousand in the early nineteenth century) to islands in the Platte River where they fattened on prairie cordgrass in preparation for the migration to the western plains. There, like the Blackfeet and other bison hunters to the north, they would find in river valleys cottonwood forage for their horses, and shelter, wood, water, and bison for themselves. They stayed in these winter havens for months at a time, killing bison, drying meat and tanning hides, feasting, and telling stories. The Pawnees had no official ceremonies in winter; their ceremonies ended in October when the animals hibernated and the world went into dormancy.

At the beginning of March, the Pawnees returned to their silent villages, carrying parfleches of dried bison meat to be used in the spring ceremonies that ushered in the agricultural year. The grass was sure to sprout green around the villages, providing rich pasture for the horses, because the Pawnees would have burned the prairie before leaving on the winter hunt. Soon the stars and animals would indicate that it was time to plant, and so began another round in the cycle of Pawnee life.

Textures of Life

How well did these ecologically adjusted cycles, repeating year after year in familiar lands, work in terms of providing satisfactory standards of living for the Plains Indians? How sound was their subsistence base? How were the different Indian nations connected through trading? How did their social systems function to foster cohesion and accommodate stress? And what were the distinctive roles of men and women in keeping the cycles turning smoothly?

Early European and American assessments of the well-being of the Indians varied greatly, depending on time and place. This is hardly surprising given the fluctuating extremes of the Great Plains environment, with its driving blizzards and desiccating summers, violent hailstorms and apocalyptic grasshopper infestations, all of which affected crops, bison migrations, and the availability of plants to collect. Add to these natural hazards introduced diseases that could take a society to the brink of extinction almost overnight, and the constant state of warfare, which took a terrible toll, especially on young men, and also disrupted subsistence activities.

The trader James Mackay, exploring the upper Missouri for Spain in the summer of 1795, was greatly impressed by the fertility of the soil and the healthy disposition of the Indians who, he claimed, were afflicted by "very few Diseases," other than those introduced by Europeans. Yet only the previous November, another Spanish trader, Jean Baptiste Truteau, was in winter camp near the mouth of the Niobrara when hundreds of Omahas, "half dead with hunger," staggered in. Truteau learned that their corn crop had failed and the nation had been forced to disperse in small bands along the Missouri bottoms, seeking subsistence where they could. The Omahas' situation only got worse when they were struck by a devastating smallpox epidemic in the winter of 1800–1801. By the time Lewis and Clark passed by in 1804, the Omahas, with their population reduced by more than a half, had abandoned and burned their Nebraska village and had become a "wandering nation" living off the land.

Generally, however, the traders and explorers were impressed by the Indians' agriculture. In August of 1803, for example, the perceptive North West Company trader Charles McKenzie had only praise for the cornucopia of crops raised at the Mandan-Hidatsa villages:

> I never witnessed anything equal in richness to the appearance of the fields—the Stalks of the Indian corn were generally eight feet high;-the leaves of the Kidney beans were entirely covered with blossoms, promising abundance. The pumpkins were already gathered, cut into Slices, dried in the Sun, and ready for use.

Another North West Company trader, Alexander Henry, was also impressed (in 1805) by the "immense quantity of corn, beans, squashes, tobacco" grown at the Mandan villages. And the English explorer John Bradbury, himself a botanist, commented in 1811 that he had never seen anywhere corn "in finer order, or better managed" than at the Arikara villages. Bradbury also noted their fine stands of squashes, beans, and tobacco.

The European visitors, as well as the Indians themselves, reaped the benefit of these prolific harvests: in 1806, at the Hidatsa village, Henry and his fellow North West Company traders were regaled with a bounty of "fresh and dried fruit, sweet corn prepared in different manners, green pumpkins and beans, meats green and dried."

The credit for this agricultural success accrued to the Indian women who, as Bradbury recognized, were "excellent cultivators." Edwin James, chronicler of the Stephen Long expedition, which passed through the Pawnee villages on its way to the Rocky Mountains in 1820, captured the bustling morning scene in the planting season: "As soon as the day dawned," he wrote, "we observed the surrounding plain, filled with groups of [Indian women] trooping to the cornfields in every direction." Some of them stopped to look at the strange Americans, but James saw that "the air of serious business was manifest in their circumstances, and they soon hurried away to their daily labors." Add to this evocation the melee of dogs that always accompanied the women to the fields, and perhaps a few young men who had volunteered to go along for protection (and flirtation), and here is a panorama of the performance of daily life in spring in Indian villages up and down the eastern Great Plains.

The women's farming practices made sound ecological sense. Their flint corns, carefully nurtured and protected, were hardy, drought-resistant, and able to withstand the hailstorms that are a factor of life on the Great Plains. Their fields were covered by a carpet of intersown crops that protected the soil and conserved the moisture. And when a field was drained of its fertility after a few years of use, the women simply shifted their efforts to a new plot with its untouched stores of humus.

But expertise and effort could only accomplish so much in a land of periodic drought. Prince Maximilian, the great German naturalist who traveled up the Missouri in 1833, was a witness to this: he was greatly impressed by the farming skills of the Indian women and their bounty of crops, but he also observed that sometimes "in the heat of the summer the creeks become dry and the crops of maize . . . fail in consequence of the drought."

When this happened, there was always bison, deer, and other game as well as the variety of collected foods to rely upon. These, of course, were the only means of subsistence of the bison hunters.

There was a seemingly inexhaustible supply of bison at the beginning of the nineteenth century. In the summer of 1805, Charles McKenzie described how the plains near the Mandan-Hidatsa villages were "so thickly covered with Buffalos that we were often under the necessity of frightening them out of our way by means of Gunpowder;" at night the traders were "in constant dread of being overrun and crushed by them."

That same summer, McKenzie's North West Company colleague, the young Frenchman François-Antoine Larocque, climbed a hill near the Little Missouri River and, looking out, saw "as far as the Eye could discern," bison "in amazing number." In such situations, bison were just there for the taking by the mounted Indians; as Larocque noted, referring specifically to the Crows, "they find no difficulty in finding provision for a numerous family."

But in winter the herds could sometimes be localized, distant, and unobtainable. There was also the issue of winterkill. In April of 1800, for example, after a hard, cold winter, Alexander Henry came across a field of fallen bison "so weak," he wrote, "that if they lie down they cannot rise."

The village Indians, however, may well have wished for such harsh winters because in those conditions bison would pour into the Missouri River valley, seeking shelter from the winds. McKenzie was on hand to see such a scene near the main Hidatsa village in 1804, and he described it in his journal:

"About Christmas," he wrote, "the Buffalos drew near the villages, and we lived off the fat of the land. Hunting and eating became the order of the day." McKenzie related how "multitudes" of bison tried to cross the frozen Missouri and fell through the ice and drowned. In spring the banks of the river were "littered with rotting carcasses." McKenzie described this aged meat as being "so green and ripe and tender" that it hardly needed cooking. It was, he wrote, "preferred by the Indians to any other type of food." In fact, the Mandans would actually bury dead bison in the fall and exhume the putrid meat for consumption in the spring. The traders were not so convinced that this was a delicacy.

In recent times, much has been made of the Indian as an ecological model, living in balance with nature, a potential antidote to the violence that modern societies wreak on the environment. And it is true that much can be learned from the Indians' humility toward nature, their sense of respect and awe, their understanding that they were just one small part of it. But there was nothing conservationist about the way they hunted bison. They did indeed use just about all the parts of the bison, but they did not use all the parts of *every* bison. McKenzie, continuing his Christmas story of the bison gathering in the Missouri River valley, observed this: "Large parties went in pursuit of the buffaloes, often killing herds, but returned with only the tongues." Coyotes and wolves disposed of the rest.

This was not an isolated example. Larocque, on his way to the Yellowstone to establish trading with the Crows in the summer of 1805, was astounded at the great number of "Buffaloes and other Quadrupeds" the Indians killed. He commented that "when hunting they take but the fattest and cut part of an animal and leave the remainder." A year later, McKenzie, out on the Cannonball River with the Cheyennes, witnessed "even greater slaughter upon Buffalo" than he had seen at the Missouri: "within 20 acres of their camp," he wrote, the Cheyennes killed "250 fat cows which they left on the field as they fell, excepting the Tongues which they dried for a general feast." Such examples of wholesale overkill could be repeated for other Indians, at many other places and times.

By taking only the bison cows and calves (for both meat and robes) and selecting only the preferential cuts of humps, ribs, and tongues and leaving the rest on the ground, the Indians were clearly contradicting any contemporary sense of conservation. But contemporary understandings are irrelevant here. To the Indians the bison had always been there, and, in their cosmology, as long as they conducted their ceremonies (to which many of the bison tongues were dedicated) properly and with due respect, the bison would continue to be there, regardless of how many they killed. This is only one example (sports mascots, place names, and Hollywood Indians are others) of how Americans have manufactured a fabricated Indian to serve a purpose for themselves in the present.

When their crops dried to straw in the fields and the bison herds were absent, the Indians fell back on their rich repertoire of collected foods. And when their crops thrived in the fields and the bison were there for the taking, collected foods added nutritional balance and variety of taste to their diets. Plants were also collected for a diversity of other uses, for medicine, construction, manufacturing, and adornment.

In the early twentieth century, botanist Melvin Gilmore, drawing from the knowledge of old Indians whom he interviewed, identified more than a hundred plants that were commonly used by the farming and hunting peoples of the upper Missouri. In addition to staple foods like prairie potatoes and ground nuts, the Indians collected various fungi like elm cap, tree ears, corn smut, and puff balls, all of which were eaten when young and tender. Black walnuts, hickory nuts, and hazelnuts were gathered and made into soups, or eaten with honey. The Indians also made sugar from the sap of maples and box elders, and they stewed red root to make a tea-like drink. In times of scarcity, prickly pear cactus was roasted and eaten, after first removing the spines and stems.

The Indians drew just as widely from Great Plains' vegetation for medicinal purposes. The fruits and leaves of the cedar were boiled together to treat coughs in both humans and horses. Cedar twigs were also burned and used as a smoke treatment for nervousness and bad dreams. Calumus root was valued as a decoction for fever and colic and chewed to relieve colds and toothache. In fact, according to Gilmore, calumus root was "regarded as a panacea" for illness. Wild four-o'clock root (called by the Omahas and Poncas *makan-wasek*, or "strong medicine") was boiled and used to rid the body of tapeworms or used as a paste applied to wounds. The Pawnees, at least, mixed meadow rue and white clay and stuffed it in their horses' nostrils to work as a stimulant when long journeys had to be made. Pasque flower, one of the first plants to bloom in the spring, relieved the pains of rheumatism, and butterfly weed was eaten raw to help cure bronchial problems. Of course, none of these ingenious curatives, a natural pharmacology worked out over generations, were to any avail in the treatment of deadly introduced diseases like smallpox and cholera.

A variety of trees were used for lodge construction and manufactured products. Lodgepole pines, growing in the Black Hills, on the eastern side of the Bighorns, and at the headwaters of Lodgepole Creek in the Laramie Range, were sought for use as tipi poles, and American elms provided the sturdy posts that supported the earth lodges. Elm was also used to make massive corn mortars and pestles. Indians would go out of their way to find stands of ash for arrows and pipe stems, and long trips were made to Oklahoma to find Osage orange trees, which furnished the very best wood for bows.

Beyond the necessities of subsistence, health, and shelter was a selection of wild plants that were used for comfort and personal presentation. The down of the cattail worked as a diaper for babies and as a filling for pillows. Seeds of wild columbine were crushed and rubbed on clothes and the body as a fragrance. The fruits of meadow rue, with their delicate pine-like odor, were used in the same way. Among the Omahas, men used the crushed fruits of the prickly ash shrub as a perfume, and women applied dried lady's bouquet as a scent. Some plants, like pursh, went beyond fragrance and worked as a love charm to attract the person of one's desire. Yucca (soapweed) was used for washing hair, and wild sage was boiled down into a concentrate for bathing, which the Crows, for instance, did every morning in the river, even when they had to break through the ice in winter.

What could not be obtained self-sufficiently by farming, hunting, and food collection in home territories could be acquired through exchange in trade networks that spanned the Great Plains, and reached far beyond. Before European goods filtered in, this was an exchange of products of the hunt for products of the soil, especially at the trade mecca of the Mandan and Hidatsa villages, and at a subsidiary hub at the Arikara villages, a little lower down the Missouri. There was also the Comanche-dominated trade nexus at the Big Timbers on the upper Arkansas River, where Indians from all over the Great Plains converged to obtain horses, especially in the winter months.

By 1803 the Cheyennes had taken on the role of the main long-distance traders, ferrying horses north from the Comanches to the Mandans, but Shoshonis, Crows, Pawnees, and Kiowas were also active in the trade. Guns and other products of the nascent Industrial Revolution were funneled by British and French traders south to the Mandans and Hidatsas, by Spanish and then American traders up to the Missouri, and, on the southern Great Plains, by French and American traders via Wichita middlemen to the Comanches. The Euro-American traders quickly discovered that they had to fit into the existing system, with its own geopolitics and protocols, and deal with Indian traders who were just as shrewd and profit-motivated as themselves. As Larocque said of the Crows, "They know well how to make an advantageous bargain in their sales and purchases."

Each Indian group tried to capitalize on the geographic variations in supply and demand, especially involving guns and horses. The Crows, for example, got their horses from the Flatheads, who had so many (horses were also channeled up the west side of the Rockies) that they exchanged them, as Larocque put it, "for a trifle." Then, as Larocque explained, the Crows passed them on at the Mandan and Hidatsa villages "at double the price they paid for them." The Mandans and Hidatsa raised the price again as they traded the horses to the Assiniboines, who in turn moved them on at a profit to the Crees. Guns flowed in the other direction, transferred at a profit at each stage to the west.

When French, British, and American traders appeared on the scene, they were both courted and resisted by the Indians: courted, because all the Indians wanted guns and manufactured products that made their lives easier; resisted, because they did not want the traders to bypass them and supply guns to their rivals, which would not only prevent them from profiting on the exchange but also sway the balance of power against them. So the Wichitas tried, in vain, to prevent American traders from going directly to the Comanches; the Kansa, Otoes, Omahas, and Arikaras each tried, in succession, to stop

Spanish and American traders from moving up the Missouri River with their stocks of guns; and, as Larocque discovered on his way to the Mandans, the Assiniboines had a "fixed determination to prevent . . . as much as they can, any Communication between traders and the Missouri Indians, as they wish to Engross that trade themselves." When Larocque and McKenzie reached the Mandan and Hidatsa villages, they found that those Indians in turn were reluctant to allow them to open up a direct trade with the Crows, because it would eliminate their profitable middleman role. But there was no stopping the Euro-American traders because the profits were greatest where the trade goods were scarcest. As McKenzie noted in his journal, "I know that my goods would bring a better price at the Shawyens [Cheyennes] than they would have at the Missouri." As a result of this compelling economics, all the Indian nations of the central and northern Great Plains would have a trading post by 1832.

The main trading season on the upper Missouri was summer, when the crops of the village Indians were ripe to harvest. Massive trading parties of bison hunters would come down to the Mandan-Hidatsa villages. Charles McKenzie was on hand to witness such a spectacular scene in the summer of 1805, and he left this vivid description:

> About the middle of June the Rocky Mountain Indians [Crows] made their appearance. They consisted of more than three hundred Tents, and presented the handsomest sight that one could imagine—all on horseback. Children of small sizes were lashed to the Saddles, and those above the age of six could manage a horse . . . There were a great many horses for the baggage, and the whole exceeding two thousand covered a large space of ground and had the appearance of an army.

When trading parties came together like this, even if they had a persistent enmity, they established an atmosphere conducive to trading by participating in the calumet ceremony, which McKenzie accurately described as the "ceremony of adoption." The two parties would smoke the "pipe of social union," thereby establishing fictional kinship ties for the duration of the stay. The ritual was accompanied by days of singing, dancing, smoking, and feasting, and then by gift-giving (in effect, reciprocal trading) on a large scale. McKenzie, for example, watched the Hidatsas present the Crows with "200 guns, 100 rounds ammo, 100 bushels of corn" and a large quantity of "mercantile items," such as kettles, axes, and cloth. In return, the Crows offered 250 horses, "large parcels" of bison robes, and leather leggings and shirts "in great abundance." The Crows and Hidatsas would have had no difficulty negotiating this exchange because they had once been a single people and they spoke dialects of the same language. But when diverse groups came together to trade, they could communicate too, because they had a lingua franca, the elaborate system of more than eighty hand gestures that constituted Plains Indian sign language.

Many of the cultural practices that the traders were obliged to observe, in order to secure their profits, must have been puzzling to them. For example, Indians were accustomed to dressing in their finest regalia to trade, their brilliant appearance expressing their importance. So when Alexander Henry and another North West Company trader turned up at the Hidatsa village in June of 1806 in bedraggled and water-damaged clothes, the Indians wouldn't take them seriously because of the "meanness of their appearance." In general, as McKenzie explained, the Indians were "accustomed to look upon every white man as inferior to themselves."

The Plains Indians had devised their social systems over generations to ensure that not only trade but all the year's activities proceeded as smoothly as possible. Again, there was great variation in social organization across the region, the main distinction, perhaps, being the contrast between the system of hereditary leadership among the village Indians and the more fluid organization of the decentralized bison hunters: as the Tetons (one of the three main divisions of the Sioux) told Truteau in 1795, they "did not have one chief greater than all the others," but that "each man was a chief in his lodge." Even among the village Indians a chief had to earn his position through acts of courage and generosity and by displaying wisdom. And in both sets of cases, the band was the main social unit, and a band was essentially an extended family. The Cheyennes, for example, were structured into ten bands, each of which was represented on the tribal council by four chiefs, and the Omahas were made up of ten clans, each with its own responsibilities in the functioning of life. Other institutions, such as age-graded men's societies, also fostered cohesion, as did a shared language and religion.

Within each society, decision-making was by consensus and aimed at the common good. Reciprocal sharing ensured a basic social security: as Truteau observed of the Arikaras, each "prided himself on helping his neighbour, whether it be for food or other necessities." If a man died, his wife, or wives (multiple wives, often sisters, were the norm) would likely be taken in by a brother.

Personal disputes were generally settled quietly, as Larocque explained, by "a present of a horse or a gun ... to the offended person, as a means of reconciliation." But if an offense jeopardized the stability of the society, then punishment could be severe. According to Larocque, if anyone violated the protocols of the bison hunt, by making a premature attack, for example, they were "punished by a beating or their arms were broken, and their tents were cut to pieces."

In these communal societies, however, there was plenty of latitude for individualism, even in religious expression. Larocque noted that while "the sun, moon, stars, heaven and earth" were universally venerated, it was a person's own particular dreams "that cause him to worship one thing rather than another."

There was also choice and tolerance in the expression of gender roles. Many of the Plains Indian societies recognized and honored a third gender, male berdaches, or "two spirited" men, who chose to do women's work, dressed as women, and had relations with non-berdache men. Rather than being ostracized for their preferences, berdaches were respected for their special insights, as well as for skills such as quillwork and beading. Similarly, some Indian women chose to dress like men and to follow men's roles, aspiring to become notable warriors.

Euro-American observers, like Thompson, McKenzie, Larocque, and Truteau, and subsequently missionaries and Indian agents, rarely failed to comment that Indian women did nearly all the manual labor, and that Indian men were "lazy." Here is Larocque, for example, characterizing the Crows: "Like all other Indian nations the women do most of the work . . . while the men are proportionately idle." Larocque conceded that the men did indeed kill the bison, but he stressed that "their wives who generally follow them skin the Animal, and dress it while they [the men] sit looking by." The Crow men, Larocque continued, "do not even saddle their own horses when their wives are present." Larocque considered it fortuitous for the women that the Crows had plenty of horses; otherwise they would have had to do all the carrying. The situation was no different at the villages, where, as McKenzie observed, "the men never trouble themselves about the labours of the fields, unless to reprimand the women for some noted neglect, and sow a few squares of tobacco."

It is true that the women did most of the diurnal labor at the villages and encampments. In addition to farming and dressing hides (a labor-intensive activity), they built the earth lodges, often hauling heavy timber from a distance, made and erected the tipis, collected wild plants, cooked all the food, carried the tipis, carried the water, and much more. They also lacked society-wide political power (you will look in vain for a woman's signature on a nineteenth century treaty), and while they played active roles in religious ceremonies, it was generally the men who were in charge. Lives of constant toil, and frequent child-bearing, meant that Indian women often died at an early age.

But looked at more closely, it can be seen that Indian men and women had complementary roles in their societies, for which they were equally respected. The men's work took place not at the villages but out on the open plains, hunting bison and raiding for horses and glory at dawn. Their prescribed roles were so dangerous that they died at even younger ages, and in greater numbers, than the women. David Thompson was one of the first to notice the prevailing demographic imbalance in Plains Indian societies, and he wrote, concerning the Piegans, that the "grown-up population of these people appear to be about three men to every five women. . . ." This lopsided Plains Indians demography persisted until the end of the war-torn nineteenth century. In 1840, for example, 59 percent of the adults in the Pawnee Confederation were women; thirty years of turmoil later and the discrepancy was even greater: 63 percent of the adults were women, and the total number of adults was much smaller. Clearly, each gender had its part to play in a life that was often lived close to the bone.

Indian women had their own forms of power too. They owned the earth lodge and tipi, and an abusive husband might be expelled, taking only his weapons with him. Women owned the products they produced, such as crops, hide clothes, and pemmican, and they had the right to trade them. The senior wife made most of the decisions in the lodge, and on the bison hunt women had a say in where to camp. Indian women also took care of the sacred bundles and were responsible for them on the hunt. They played a major role in healing, especially in matters concerned with childbirth. Women were also cherished as members of close, loving families. As Larocque conceded, after itemizing the Crow women's heavy workload, "the men are fond of their wives and treat them well." David Thompson came to a similar conclusion at the Mandan villages, where he observed, that "both sexes have the character of being courteous."

By 1803 these intricate textures of life were becoming torn and frayed. In subsequent decades defined by war and disease and a federal Indian policy directed at obtaining lands for Americans, the fabric of their lives would unravel. Americans would label them "savages" and "barbarians," which in their eyes justified dispossession by a "civilized" people. But some of the early traders and explorers who were eyewitnesses to traditional Indian life in all its complexity saw matters differently. Jean Baptiste Truteau, showing empathy and understanding, wrote in his journal that it was contact with "civilized ones" that caused the Indians to become "infected with their peculiar faults and vices." Truteau contrasted the civility, kindness, and humanity of Indian societies, their care for one another, with the "lack of charity" and the individual ambition and striving for wealth of the "White Men." He suggested that if the Indians knew the true disposition of Euro-Americans "and the tricks, the frauds, the crimes . . . which they practice against the rights of nature," then they "might justly apply to them the designation of savages and barbarians which we have given to them." This is a harsh indictment, but one worth following through the nineteenth century as the Plains Indians were stripped of nearly all of their lands and their traditional ways of life.

CHAPTER THREE

A Century of Dispossession

The Plains Indians started the nineteenth century with a collective land base that reached from the Canadian prairies almost to the Gulf of Mexico, and from the Missouri River to the Rocky Mountains. The United States recognized the Indians' "right of occupancy" to these lands, subject only to its own higher sovereignty that came with the Louisiana Purchase. Over the course of the nineteenth century the United States exercised its assumed superior claim to the land and bought, or took, the Indians' estate to make room for American settlers. Indian dispossession was, in effect, the first stage of the American "frontier process." Indian country had to be converted into public domain before it could be surveyed and allocated out to settlers through land laws like the Homestead Act of 1862.

The settlement, or more accurately, resettlement, of the Great Plains was so rapid in the second half of the nineteenth century that in 1890 the United States Bureau of the Census declared the frontier "closed" and the era of free land over. Two years later, historian Frederick Jackson Turner presented his landmark paper, "The Significance of the Frontier in American History," celebrating the American takeover and the victory of "civilization over savagery."

By that time Indian country had been broken into numerous reservations located in two main areas (fig. 8). On the northern

Great Plains, hunting Indians like the Crows, Blackfeet, and Sioux had managed to hold on to parts of their original homelands, and the remnants of the village Indians—the Mandans, Hidatsas, and Arikaras—had been consolidated into a single reservation at Fort Berthold on the upper Missouri. On the southern Great Plains, Indians from other parts of the region, and from all over the United States, had been concentrated in Indian Territory (after 1907, Oklahoma). Even the mighty Comanches were confined there. The entire state of Texas was devoid of reservations. Texas Indians had been mercilessly killed during the Texas Republic (1836–45) and subsequently expelled during the early decades of statehood. The central Great Plains, comprising Kansas, Nebraska, and eastern Colorado, were also stripped of Indians and had few reservations: this was the cutting edge of the American advance, and the fertile prairies were deemed too valuable to remain in the hands of the original owners. Pawnees, Poncas, Otoe-Missourias, Kansa, and Osages were all rapidly surrounded by Americans after midcentury and forced to sever their roots and leave for Indian Territory.

Restricted on reservations, immured within straight lines (a new concept for the Indians, but the preferred Euro-American way to carve up space), the Plains Indians watched their familiar homelands fill up with newcomers and empty out of everything else. Most significantly, by the late 1880s the massive bison herds that had supported them had been reduced to fields of bones whitening the prairie. Overkill, disease, and competition from cattle for forage contributed to their rapid decline. Speaking in 1882, the Omaha chief Joseph La Flesche recalled a better time when he would see Indians and "think they were the only people." But then Americans came, "just as the blackbirds do, and spread over the country," filling every space. Forty years later, his compatriot,

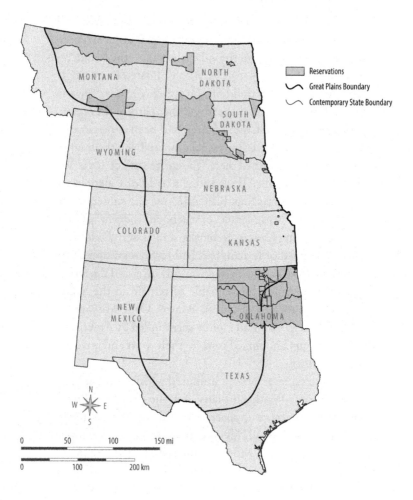

Reservations

~~ **Great Plains Boundary**

~~ **Contemporary State Boundary**

MONTANA

NORTH
DAKOTA

SOUTH
DAKOTA

WYOMING

NEBRASKA

COLORADO

KANSAS

NEW
MEXICO

OKLAHOMA

TEXAS

N
W — E
S

0   50   100   150 mi

0   100   200 km

8. American Indian reservations on the Great Plains, 1880. Created by Ezra J. Zeitler.

the holy man White Horse, offered this poignant elegy to his lost universe:

> Now the face of all the land is changed and sad. The living creatures are gone. I see the land desolate, and I suffer unspeakable sadness. Sometimes I wake in the night and feel as though I would suffocate from the pressure of this awful feeling of loneliness.

The Plains Indians had become strangers in their own land.

Federal Indian Policy and the Great Plains

After 1803, and right up to the present, the story of the Plains Indians cannot be separated from the story of the United States. The Indians continued to shape their own lives, of course, hunting bison, practicing ceremonies, venerating sacred places, and adapting in diverse ways to new conditions, but increasingly they did so in a world of other peoples' making. As American population spread west, territories, then states, were created over and above the Indians, and the squared-off township and range system extended across the Great Plains, falling like a net over country where Indians had previously moved freely. In practice, however, territories and states had very little to do with Indians (except to want them gone); then, as now, Indian policy was a federal matter run from the Indian Office, later the Bureau of Indian Affairs.

The conditions of this relationship were set in the late eighteenth and early nineteenth centuries. The United States considered the Indians to be "domestic dependent nations" and described their relationship paternalistically as that of a "guardian to a ward." Americans acknowledged the Indians' "original natural rights" but, like their European ancestors, claimed a superior right to the land through the Doctrine of Discovery, which maintained that the Indians' legal title was "impaired" by the arrival on the scene of a Christian, civilized people. This legal invention, more mighty than the sword, gave Congress plenary, or absolute, power over the Indians, including the right to obtain their lands through treaties and, if necessary at a later date, to repeal those treaties.

The main objective of federal Indian policy on the Great Plains, and throughout the country, was to obtain lands for Americans. Here is Commissioner of Indian Affairs Charles Mix, for example, writing in his annual report in 1867: "The plea of 'manifest destiny' is paramount and the Indian must give way though it may be at the sacrifice of what must be as dear as life." This sentiment was repeated by Commissioner Francis Walker in 1872: "The westward course of population is neither to be denied or delayed for all the Indians that ever called this country home. They must yield or perish." Such sentiments, expressing an ingrained American ideology that Indians were anachronisms standing in the way of progress, were repeated again and again in commissioners' reports, in Congress, and in the press.

From the time of Jefferson on, however, there was a secondary, ostensibly humanitarian, objective of federal Indian policy. President Jefferson, a true disciple of the Enlightenment and believer in the inherent capacity of all humankind, was convinced that Indians could be transformed and accelerated through the "stages of society" to become on a par with Americans. The goal of this civilization, or assimilation, policy was to settle the Indians on allotments, small plots of land like homesteads, where they would farm and become self-sufficient. In this way, Indians would disappear as a separate factor in American society, the remainder of their lands (the vast majority) would be freed-up for settlers, and Americans could take over an already occupied continent while maintaining the moral high ground. The deal was an exchange of land for "civilization," and, perversely, it was offered as a favor.

The optimistic expectations of Americans like Jefferson that the Indians could be assimilated within a generation were dashed by events on the frontier. The Indians were not willing to jettison their lands and lifestyles for duties that the men, especially, considered arduous and unexciting. They were, in any case, convinced of the rightness of their own ways of life. It was also clear that contact with Americans led to the Indians' debasement, not "improvement," as disease, alcohol, and hostilities wreaked havoc with their lives. So while the ultimate goal remained assimilation, federal policy makers fell back on the expediency of temporary segregation. Indians were repeatedly moved away from the frontier and its manifest vices and restricted to smaller and smaller tracts of land where the assimilation program was applied with increasing intensity: spatial restriction became the main means of social control. First, in the 1820s and 1830s, Indians from the eastern United States were coerced into relocating to west of the Mississippi, where they were guaranteed new, permanent homelands. Then, after the Kansas-Nebraska Act of 1854 opened up most of the Great Plains to American settlers, this "permanent Indian frontier" was shattered into multiple reservations. Finally, after 1870 (and culminating in the General Allotment Act, or Dawes Act, of 1887), the United States made a concerted push for assimilation by imposing allotments on the Indians and opening up the remaining reservation lands to settlers.

At each stage, the flood of American settlers inundated the Indians before they could make the social and cultural adjustments that were being demanded of them. The effects of the contact with Americans and the loss of traditional means of support were catastrophic. The Pawnees, Arikaras, Mandans, and Hidatsas all lost more than 90 percent of their populations over the course of the nineteenth century. By 1900 only 253 Mandans, 211 Kansa, and 706 Pawnees remained. The bison hunters, more remote from the mass of Americans and more dispersed, which tended to minimize the impact of contagious disease, fared a little better, with population losses of 85 percent for the Comanches, 70 percent for the Crows, and 50 percent for the Blackfeet. At the end of the nineteenth century it seemed likely that many Plains Indian nations were heading to extinction.

Modern terms like *genocide*, *ethnic cleansing*, and *cultural genocide* have recently been used to categorize federal Indian policy and its disastrous impact. But these terms need to be applied cautiously, because each has a precise legal meaning, and to use them indiscriminately distorts the way that history took place and is remembered.

Genocide, as defined in the 1948 Convention on Genocide, with the shadow of the Holocaust still looming, is restricted to the *physical* annihilation of a group of people. Many scholars consider this too narrow a construction, but the strict definitional focus on physical genocide (as in Rwanda in 1994) has not changed. Physical annihilation of Native Americans was not the policy of the United States. Arguably, this was because the United States did not have the military means (or the financial means) to conduct a campaign of genocide. But mainly it was because the United States wanted to achieve the supersession of Native Americans in ways that preserved its self-proclaimed reputation as an enlightened society. There were genocidal acts, of course, inexcusable atrocities like those at Sand Creek on November 29, 1864, and Wounded Knee on December 29, 1890, both of which saw Americans murder hundreds of Indian men, women, and children. These massacres were not the direct result of federal policy, however, but of an American frontier out of control, and they were condemned at the time. Moreover, the Indian Office took steps to prevent Indian deaths, as in the 1830s when Congress funded a smallpox vaccination program that led to the immunization of 54,000 Indians, mainly children, on the central Great Plains. These included 870 Pawnees, mostly infants, who were vaccinated after the terrible smallpox epidemic of 1837, and for the Pawnees smallpox was never again the scourge it had been.

The term *ethnic cleansing*, first defined during the Bosnian war of 1992–95 as the forcible removal of a population to make room for others, is much more applicable to the dispossession of the Plains Indians. The entire state of Texas was ethnically cleansed, and the restriction of the bison hunters of the western Great Plains to reservations in the 1860s and 1870s through campaigns of total war against winter camps filled with women and children clearly fits the definition of ethnic cleansing. But the removal of the Pawnees from Nebraska to Indian Territory in 1873–75, which has been labeled ethnic cleansing, was more complicated than that. The Indian Office actually wanted the Pawnees to remain in Nebraska, individualized on allotments; but the Pawnees, surrounded by settlers, preyed on by the Sioux, and mired in poverty, met in council and, against the wishes of their agent, decided to leave for Indian Territory. Ethnic cleansing was widespread in the dispossession of Plains Indians, but not every case fits the definition.

Without a doubt, however, the United States explicitly and universally practiced a policy of cultural genocide in its dealings with Plains Indians (and with Indians everywhere in the country). This was the unapologetic goal of the assimilation policy: to make Indians disappear by attacking their cultural memory, by breaking down the communal nature of their societies, by changing the roles of Indian men and women (putting the former in the fields and the latter in the home), by instilling a sense of private property and a Protestant work ethic, and by giving them a competitive drive and, as was often said, "a sense of selfishness." And when this didn't work for Indian adults, the Indian Office turned its attention to the children, who were placed in reservation and off-reservation schools, draconian places where they were taught to reject all they had known. This policy of cultural genocide, which persisted until the 1930s and has sometimes resurfaced since, caused great cultural damage, including the loss of many traditions, and resulted in population declines that were almost as great as if it had been physical genocide.

Prelude to Dispossession

There were few Americans in the Great Plains before the Kansas-Nebraska Act of 1854 opened the floodgates to settlers. Most, maybe as many as one thousand by the 1830s, were fur traders who depended on cheap Indian labor to furnish furs and robes and who, therefore, wanted the Indians to continue living traditionally. By contrast, the few hundred missionaries and Indian agency employees were in the Great Plains expressly to change the Indians. The missionaries—mainly Presbyterians, Baptists, and Methodists—came to spread the Gospel and, in their minds, rescue the Indians from their "state of darkness." To them, Christianity and civilization went hand in hand. The agents, assigned to a single Indian nation, or group of nations, were there to put the government's assimilation policy into practice as well as to maintain peace and eventually arrange the acquisition of Indian lands. Ironically, given the contrasting objectives, in the first half of the nineteenth century the traders may have changed Indian lives more than either the missionaries or the Indian agents.

Arguably, the fur trade was the best relationship Plains Indians ever had with the United States. The traders didn't want their lands and didn't ask them to change their ways, except to step up fur production. Traders often lived with the Indians, learned their languages, and married Indian women; in effect, it was a reverse, voluntary, assimilation process.

Both sides were satisfied with the economic exchange of the fur trade. Trappers like Zenas Leonard were astounded to find that to "get a beaver skin from these people [the Shoshoni] worth eight or ten dollars never cost more than an awl, a fish hook, a knife, a string of beads, or something equally as trifling." But the Indians, in turn, were astounded that a beaver pelt, of no great utility to them, was worth a gun or another extraordinary piece of Euro-American technology. This was noted by LeBorgne, an influential Hidatsa chief, in a speech reported by the trader Charles McKenzie in 1805: "White men love Beaver and they are continually in search of Beaver for its Skin—What use they make of the skin I know not but they give us good things in return—they exchange it for Guns, Ammunition, etc."

The Indians were discriminating traders and not easily duped. According to Edwin Denig, a trader from 1837 to 1855 at Fort Union at the mouth of the Yellowstone, the Crows would accept "only the very finest and highest priced goods" in return for their equally fine robes and leather products. Denig explained that "the nature of the barter for robes and other skins is such that the Indian receives what he considers an equivalent for his labor or he would not hunt." If this was exploitation, then each side was exploiting the other.

But the fur trade, so eagerly embraced by the Indians, also undermined their lives. They became participants in the destruction of their own resource base, and, without furs to trade, they could not acquire guns and ammunition, which put them at a great disadvantage in warfare. This is what happened to the village Indians of the lower Missouri—Kansa, Otoe-Missouria, Omaha, and Ponca—in the 1830s. Beaver were quickly eliminated by overtrapping, and the bison herds withdrew to the west under pressure from the fur trade. The fur traders moved on to new areas of production, such as Blackfeet country, leaving the Indians of the lower Missouri with needs, not least for guns, and no way to satisfy them.

Most disastrously, the fur trade became a conduit for the passage of disease through Indian societies. This was not in the interest of the traders, of course, because the Indians were their producers, and often their families. But short-term profits were paramount in the business of the fur trade, and in 1837 this resulted in one of the worst smallpox outbreaks in a century of recurring epidemics.

In the summer of 1837, the American Fur Company's steamboat, the *St. Peters*, made its annual voyage up the Missouri carrying merchandise to the trading posts. On board were Indian passengers infected with smallpox. The American Fur Company, which by this time had a virtual monopoly of the trade on the upper Missouri, realized that smallpox was onboard but did not want to turn back and jettison a year's trade. Instead, smallpox was unloaded with the passengers and trade goods at every stop.

By mid-July the Mandans had been infected, and the scourge soon spread to the nearby Arikara and Hidatsa villages. In August a Mandan war party clashed with the Sioux and passed on the epidemic. Despite the terrible consequences, the steamboat continued up to Fort Union. There, efforts had been made to inoculate the Indians and to warn the Assiniboines to keep their distance from the post. But the Assiniboines, bent on receiving their trade goods, came in anyway. They contracted smallpox and carried it into Canada. Soon the Blackfeet had the disease, and it raged among them throughout the autumn. The threat was taken seriously by the Crows, who fled the environs of their post, Fort Cass on the Bighorn River, and avoided the worst of the disease.

Smallpox continued its destructive path in all directions. In late 1837, a Pawnee war party engaged the Sioux and carried the infection back to their villages. About a quarter of the Pawnees died, including almost all the children who had been born after the previous epidemic in 1831. In all, according to the Commissioner of Indian Affairs, 17,200 Plains Indians perished. As the trader Jacob Halsey callously wrote, "Our most profitable Indians have died."

No group was hit harder by this epidemic than the Mandans, who were virtually eliminated in the space of a few months. Francis Chardon, the trader at their post, Fort Clark, kept a chilling journal of the effects of the disease. He first mentioned smallpox on July 14, 1837, a week after the arrival of the steamboat at Fort Clark. The disease rapidly spread among the Mandans, and soon the landscape was draped with bodies and suffused with the smell of death. The Mandans rightly blamed the traders. On July 30, 1837, the Mandan warrior, Four Bears, his "face rotten" with smallpox, urged his people to "rise all together and Not leave one of them alive." Chardon and the other traders feared for their lives, but in truth the Mandans were too sick to act. Many of them committed suicide to put an end to the suffering. One woman killed her two children, then hanged herself. Another Indian, overseen by a trader, vaccinated his infected child by cutting into his body and inserting a scab from a smallpox survivor into the wounds. The child lived. But most Mandans didn't: by the end of August, five hundred had died.

The horror continued through the fall and winter. On September 30, Chardon estimated that seven-eighths of the Mandans had died, and half of the Arikaras. By November, the usually mordant Chardon seemed to be at a loss for words to describe the destruction. He did note that the disease was "still raging" at the Hidatsa villages on March 14. After the disease waned in the spring, the Indians continued dying but now of starvation. By the end of the pestilence, the Mandans, only recently the great farmers and merchants of the northern Great Plains, were left with just sixty-three adults and about sixty children.

Smallpox epidemics would continue to devastate the Plains Indians throughout the century, though their effects were gradually mitigated by inoculation and acquired immunity. But there were always epidemics of measles, whooping cough, influenza, and cholera to take their place. On average, an epidemic of some type swept over the Great Plains about every six years during the nineteenth century; a particular Indian group was afflicted about every ten to fifteen years by a serious epidemic. In time, later on in the nineteenth century, diseases of poor living conditions, especially tuberculosis, would account for most of the deaths. For the Indians, the Great Plains, which once had supported so much life, had become a zone of death.

The fur traders also introduced a new item, alcohol, into Indian lives. It quickly became an integral part of the trading process, especially in the gift-giving rituals that accompanied the exchange. Some Indians, such as the Pawnees and Crows, seem to have kept alcohol at a distance in the early nineteenth century because they knew the violence it caused, but they were the exceptions. Alcohol was the catalyst in the disintegration of Otoe-Missouria society in the 1830s and 1840s, for example, and, according to Kenneth McKenzie, head trader at Fort Union in the early 1830s, "no liquor no trade" was the "prevailing sentiment" among the Indians.

The United States tried to control the flow of alcohol into Indian Country in 1832 and 1834 by setting up inspection stations along the Missouri River at Westport, Leavenworth, and

Council Bluffs. But it was to no avail; it was all about profits. In 1832 sixty-one gallons of alcohol were stockpiled at Fort Clark, and forty-four barrels of various alcohols were on hand at Fort Union. Access to alcohol would only get easier after 1854 when the settlers crowded in around the reservations.

The missionaries of various denominations who filed into the Great Plains in the 1820s and 1830s had nothing but contempt for the traders, whom they considered as uncivilized as, and more unscrupulous than, the Indians. Baptist missionaries accompanied the Cherokees on their forced march to Indian Territory in 1838. The Jesuit, Pierre-Jean De Smet—"Black Robe" to the Indians—established a mission for the Potawatomies at Council Bluffs in 1838 and then traveled the length and breadth of the northern Great Plains, baptizing Indian children. The Blackfeet called him "the man who talks to the Great Spirit." And, to give another example from many, Presbyterian John Dunbar was sent by the American Board for Foreign Missions to live with the Pawnees in 1834. Dunbar brought his wife and children to Nebraska to serve as a model of the Christian nuclear family that he hoped the Pawnees would emulate.

Despite the denominational diversity, the missionaries' goals were essentially the same: to spread the Gospel and thereby rescue the "benighted" Indians from their condition of "depravity" and "darkness." Teaching the Indians English, using the Scriptures as texts, became an integral part of the program. The missionaries found that this was a slow process, so some learned Indian languages and used them in sermons to convey the Christian message. Moral training was an integral part of the message: This involved instilling in the Indians the values of American society, such as a work ethic, individualism, and monogamy. The missionaries especially targeted Indian children in their schools, hoping to transform them before traditional habits took hold. Although there were debates over which should come first, Christianization or civilization, in essence the two were fused.

All the missionaries were offended by the Indians' ways of life: the men's apparent idleness and the women's seeming enslavement, the practice of polygamy, the quick recourse to warfare, and their religious ceremonies, which were dismissed as superstition and excuses for gluttony. But the missionaries differed greatly in their compassion for the Indians, and even in their honesty. At the lower end of the scale, Baptist missionaries to the Ottawas in Kansas in the 1860s, in collusion with Indian agents, stole thousands of acres of Indian lands under the pretense of establishing an Indian university. At the other end of the scale were dedicated men like John Dunbar, who cared greatly for the Pawnees and lived with them for a decade in dangerous and deprived conditions and tried to protect them from the Sioux, self-serving traders, and starvation. Of course, Dunbar was as ethnocentric as the other missionaries: he admired the Pawnees as a "liberal, kind-hearted people," but he also saw them as "heathen, dark-minded heathen."

Dunbar lived with the Pawnees from 1834 to 1846, at first as a welcomed guest in their lodges, then later in a crude log house that also served as the mission. He even accompanied the Pawnees on their bison hunts, living in a tipi all winter. Dunbar was highly esteemed by the Pawnees as a holy man, in part because in his first winter with them the bison herds came as far east as their central Nebraska villages, which hadn't happened in more than twenty years. The Pawnees interpreted this as an endorsement from their own Supreme Being, Ti-ra-wa. Before long, Dunbar had learned the Chaui dialect of Pawnee and could "converse with them on most subjects." He translated parts of the Scriptures into Chaui, and used the language in his sermons. The Pawnees showed a theological interest in Dunbar's religion, but the concept of proselytizing was alien to them, and they were tenacious in their own beliefs. Their rational argument was that if Ti-ra-wa had wanted them to worship the Bible, he would have given them one; but instead they had their sacred bundles and ceremonies they had observed for generations.

Faced with the Pawnees' religious intransigence, and also their dire living conditions, Dunbar put the "spiritual good" of the Indians aside and turned his attention to their "temporal needs" (this was a transition that many of the missionaries on the Great Plains went through). He became a lay doctor, treating the Indians for diseases like measles and whooping cough, and there were always the wounds of battle to attend to. He hid Pawnee children in his mission when the Sioux raided, which became a frequent event in the 1840s. In 1844 he prevented total starvation by giving them the mission's crop of corn, after the Pawnee's harvests and bison hunts had yielded little food. But as the Sioux attacks intensified, the situation became too dangerous for Dunbar and his family. In 1846, after waiting in vain for government protection, they reluctantly left. "They will doubtless feel bad when they come to know we have left them," Dunbar wrote, and he added "their prospects are dark and as we turn away from them we commend them to Him."

Individuals like Dunbar came and went, but as a group the missionaries had come to stay. In the second half of the nineteenth century they came to dominate Indian education, and they led the attack on Indian lifestyles and beliefs. They were often appointed as Indian agents, and in that role they vigorously applied the assimilation policy. By 1900 few reservations, if any, were without a mission and a mission school. Eventually, Christianity did take root, but it was on the Indians' terms, and the new beliefs and practices were grafted onto the existing tribal religions. The great Sioux holy man, Black Elk, for example, accepted Catholicism in 1904, but he never deviated from his traditional Indian beliefs, so beautifully expressed in the 1932 book *Black Elk Speaks*.

The Geography of Dispossession

The most powerful and disruptive intervention in Plains Indians' lives in the nineteenth century were the Indian agents, the men charged with implementing the assimilation policy. Over the course of the century they curtailed Indian independence, tying them down to their reservations, forcing them to put their children in government schools, and eventually even selecting tribal leaders. Some agents were good people who cared for the Indians and did their best to protect them from the strife of American encroachment; others were mercenary and corrupt, often absent from their posts, and in the job only because it paid a good salary (and offered additional opportunities for embezzlement). Whatever their motivations, they all believed that the Indians had to give up their traditional lands and lifestyles and take up allotments or else be crushed by the "westward march of progress."

A blueprint of federal Indian policy was outlined in 1829 by John Dougherty, who was in charge of the Council Bluffs Agency, with authority over the Omahas, Otoe-Missourias, and Pawnees. Dougherty spoke their languages fluently and had their trust: "We have known him since his boyhood," the Otoe chief Ietan told William Clark, the veteran of the Lewis and Clark expedition, who, as superintendent of Indian Affairs, oversaw most of the Plains Indian agencies from 1822 to 1838. Dougherty was emphatic that the Indians had to change or perish. He proposed that they should be placed on small plots of land that could be farmed and where there was no game, "in order to wean him from his favorite pursuit [hunting] and thereby prepare his mind to encounter the laborious duties of domestic life." Blacksmiths, laborers, farmers, and implements should be furnished, so that in time the Indians would be able to "clothe and subsist themselves by individualized exertions." Once tied to place, the Indians should be "taught to read, use figures, divide the year into months and days, so that they could undertake domestic manufacture." Agriculture was the key, Dougherty concluded, to raising the Indian "one grade higher in civilization," and self-sufficiency would reduce the sums of federal money needed for their support when the game ran out. With few variations—Dougherty thought it was "worse than useless" to try to Christianize the Indians until they were settled down on allotments—this was the assimilation policy forced upon the Plains Indians in the nineteenth century.

The escalating federal presence in the Great Plains was evident in the increase in the number of agencies over time. In 1824 there were four agencies, each with jurisdiction over a number of Indian nations. By 1837 there were nine agencies, the main increase coming in Indian Territory to supervise the relocated eastern Indians—Cherokees, Creeks, Choctaws, and Chickasaws. Eleven new agencies were added from 1846 to 1859, especially in eastern Kansas and Nebraska, where the village Indians had been placed on individual reservations. By 1872 thirty-four agencies were on the Great Plains, from the Blackfeet agency in the north to the Kiowa agency in the south. After 1868 many of these agencies were run by religious organizations, in an effort to eliminate the previous rampant corruption. The Society of Friends, or Quakers, operated four agencies in Nebraska and six each in Kansas and Indian Territory. Methodists, Catholics, Episcopalians, and Presbyterians were in charge of others. This religious experiment lasted for a few years, after which the agents again became political appointees.

The proliferation of agencies went side by side with the acquisition of Indian lands. Until 1871 obtaining Indian lands was officially accomplished through treaties—bilateral agreements between sovereign entities—but with the United States' sovereignty presumed superior. In fact, according to its legal presumption, the Doctrine of Discovery, the United States had the power to take the lands unilaterally; but for pragmatic and moral reasons, most Indian lands were purchased, though for a pittance. It was always a buyer's market, because as the bison herds diminished and the Indians were reduced to penury by famine and disease, the only remaining option was to exchange their last asset, land, for American support. Negotiations took place, the Indians had their say, and the United States set the terms of the divestiture. After 1871 dispossession continued through agreements and executive orders, which were essentially substitutes for treaties, and the Indians' land base continued to diminish.

The earliest treaties—with the Osage and Kansa in 1815, the Otoes and Poncas in 1817, and the four bands of the Pawnees in 1818, all negotiated under the authority of Superintendent William Clark—used almost exactly the same language to assert peace and friendship and have the Indians acknowledge that they were now "under the protection of the United States of America and no other nation." No lands were ceded; it was a holding pattern maintaining order and authority until their country was needed.

Land cessions began in 1818, when the Quapaws sold what is now the southern half of Oklahoma for a single payment of $4,000 in goods and merchandise and annual payments of $1,000 (fig. 9). Subsequent cessions by the Osage (1818), the Kansa (1825), and the Pawnees and Otoes (1833) opened up a belt of Indian Country from the Platte River to Texas. The Kansa received a half cent an acre for their cession of fine agricultural lands in northern Kansas, the Pawnees 1.1 cent an acre for much of fertile southern Nebraska.

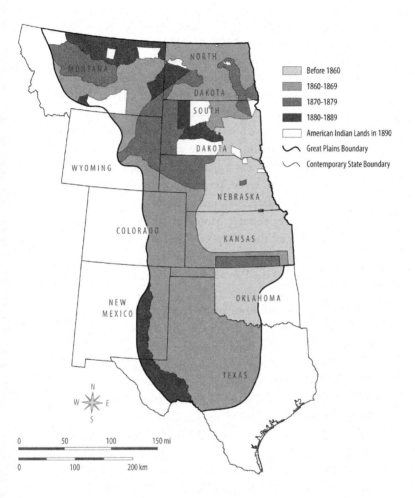

Before 1860
1860-1869
1870-1879
1880-1889
American Indian Lands in 1890
Great Plains Boundary
Contemporary State Boundary

9. American Indian land cessions on the Great Plains. Created by Ezra J. Zeitler.

These vacated lands weren't yet needed for American settlers, but they were needed for transplanted eastern Indians. By 1840 Delawares, Kickapoos, Shawnees, Ottawas, and others had been moved multiple times across the Midwest to new homes in Kansas, and about sixty thousand Creeks, Chickasaws, Seminoles, and Cherokees had been marched from the southeastern United States into Oklahoma, with about a quarter of them dying along the way. This was Jefferson's idea of the Great Plains as a giant reservation, a "permanent Indian frontier," but with Americans converging from the East, especially across Missouri and Iowa, there would be nothing permanent about it. Moreover, the indigenous Plains nations considered these imported Indians to be as foreign as Americans, and the Delawares, for example immediately became enemies of the Pawnees and Kansa, as they all competed for the bison range.

The sale of western Iowa at the Treaty of Prairie du Chien in 1830 by the eastern bands of the Sioux, Iowas, Menominees, Winnebagos, Omahas, and Otoe-Missourias serves as a case study of American buying policy in all its duplicity. The Indian delegations met with William Clark over the course of a week. They all claimed the right to hunt in western Iowa, and they fought over it. Clark told them that it was time to "bury the war tomahawk deep in the ground," or else face the U.S. Army. He persuaded the Indians to give up their "title and claim" to western Iowa, though they retained the right to hunt there peacefully. In return for the cession, the Otoe-Missourias, for example, were given an annual annuity of $2,500 for ten years and provided with the services of a blacksmith and $500 worth of farming equipment. Ietan, chief of the Otoes, pleaded with Clark to extend the annuity to twenty years, because, he said, game was increasingly scarce, and they could not support themselves by farming alone. To this Clark replied that he was sorry that the compensation disappointed them, but it was as much as the "Great Council of the Nation" (that is, Congress) would give.

There was more than a little deception involved in this treaty. Clark had assured the Indians that "we don't purchase those lands with a view to settling the white people on them," and "we think you are more benefitted by it than the Government." Yet a week later he wrote to the Commissioner of Indian Affairs that he had acquired "a disposable country of the best lands on the Missouri." The hunting rights were simply allowed to lapse, and Americans filled the vacated space in the 1840s.

This was the operative buying policy of the United States for the remainder of the nineteenth century. The Indian Office, always short of funds, obtained the lands as cheaply as possible. The average payment for the 290 million acres ceded on the central and northern Great Plains between 1825 and 1900 was ten cents an acre.

Moreover, the proceeds for the sales were not the Indians' to use. Instead, the government used the money to try to make the Indians self-sufficient (by providing the services of farmers and blacksmiths as well as agricultural equipment), so they would not need support in the future. There was a glaring contradiction here: The Indians' own money was used to fund the civilization program—to get them settled down on allotments—yet the payments given were so small that there was no chance that the policy would work. And the tactic of allowing Indians to hunt on ceded land "during the pleasure of the President," then withdrawing those rights quietly, would continue and be applied to the bison hunters in the 1860s and 1870s. The putative deal of "civilization for land" was no deal at all for the Plains Indians.

By 1850 American settlers had spread across Missouri and Iowa and were backed up against the Great Plains. The land was now needed for white settlement. Following the Kansas-Nebraska Act of 1854, the United States quickly negotiated a series of treaties with the Sisseton, Wahpeton, and Yankton bands of Sioux and the Poncas, Omahas, Pawnees, and Otoe-Missourias, thereby providing hundreds of thousands of acres of land for American settlers on the eastern Great Plains (fig. 9). The Indians were given small reservations for their "future occupancy and home," and graduated annuities that would decline over the years as the Indians, theoretically, became self-supporting on allotments. The Yanktons, for example, were paid $65,000 a year for the first ten years. This amounted to a payment of 14.1 cents an acre for southeastern South Dakota.

Payments per acre were higher in the 1850s than in the 1830s because the Indians could no longer reliably support themselves by traditional means, and the civilization program had to be intensified. Again, it was the president and his commissioners who decided how the Indians' money would be "expended for their benefit." And again, their money was applied to transforming them, to breaking down their communal societies and individualizing them on allotments. By the 1860s, their due payments would be withheld if the men did not work in the fields or if Indian children were not put in schools; in effect, their annuities became another way to control them.

Throughout the century, the United States continued to obtain Indian lands as cheaply as possible and by any means necessary. The 1863 sale of the Red River valley of the north by the Red Lake and Pembina bands of the Chippewas is another case in point. Commissioner of Indian Affairs William P. Dole appointed Minnesota governor Alexander Ramsey as chief negotiator. Dole told Ramsey to "ignore the imaginary value of the land" in setting the purchase price. Ramsey met with the Indians in a series of councils. He downplayed the agricultural potential of the land and told the Indians that this would be their last opportunity to get a good compensation. The Indians made two offers, both of which Ramsey dismissed as "extravagant and ridiculous." They finally gave in and accepted a payment of $20,000 a year for twenty years, or 8.1 cents an acre. Ramsey immediately wrote to Dole boasting how he had tricked the Chippewas by initially feigning disinterest in their land. He told Dole that in reality the soils of the valley were of "exceptional fertility," and he proudly concluded that "no territorial acquisitions of equal intrinsic value have been made from the Indians at so low a rate per acre or on terms so advantageous to the Government."

With the eastern portions of the Great Plains secured for American settlement, the United States turned its attention to the lands of the bison hunters. The decades between 1860 and 1879 saw the American acquisition of most of the western Great Plains, from the Rio Grande to the Canadian border (fig. 9). Unlike the dispossession on the eastern Great Plains, which was mainly a matter of attrition, the process on the western Great Plains was steeped in blood. Americans massacred Indians, Indians massacred Americans, and Indians massacred each other.

This violence was set against a backdrop of encroaching American settlers, who fanned out across the region, drawn along by the proliferating railroads. By 1890 Americans occupied the central Great Plains from the Missouri River to the Rocky Mountains. The eastern portions of Texas and the newly created states of North Dakota and South Dakota had also been substantially resettled.

The dispossession went hand in hand with the depletion, and almost elimination, of the bison herds. Incentives for killing bison increased after 1870 when technological innovations allowed bison hides to be processed for use as machine belts in the burgeoning factories of the East. The price for hides soared.

Also, the convergence of homesteaders onto the bison range brought a new pressure: from November to April, when the frozen meat could be transported, thousands of settlers would go west in hunting parties. They could obtain enough meat in a day to last an entire winter. The plains where the bison herds had recently thundered were now littered with skinned and partially butchered carcasses. The slaughter was rapid. In Norton County in northwestern Kansas, for example, there were still large herds along the Solomon River in 1875. A year later, they were all gone. The last bison seen in eastern Colorado was in 1887. By 1890 only about a thousand bison existed anywhere.

Conflicts between Indians and Americans escalated, with atrocities being committed by both sides. On November 29, 1864, at Sand Creek, on the windswept plains of southeastern Colorado, the crazed Methodist minister Col. John M. Chivington and his Colorado Volunteers attacked Black Kettle's peaceful village of southern Cheyennes and Arapahos, killing hundreds of Indians, mainly women and children. Eventually, more than a century later, the Methodist Church would issue an apology for this atrocity.

Farther north, from 1865 to 1867, Sioux led by Red Cloud and Crazy Horse launched attacks along the Bozeman Trail, which linked Julesburg, Colorado, on the newly constructed Union Pacific with Virginia City, Montana, where gold had been discovered in 1862. On December 21, 1866, Sioux killed eighty men under the command of Capt. William Fetterman near Fort Phil Kearney in Wyoming Territory. The conflicts would rage for more than a decade.

Meanwhile, Indians fought each other over access to the diminishing bison range. Pawnees and Sioux had been making war on each other at least since the early 1800s, as the Sioux winter counts repeatedly show. For the Pawnees it all came to a head on August 5, 1873, in a ravine in southwestern Nebraska, a place known ever since as Massacre Canyon. The Pawnees, consisting of two hundred men, a hundred women, and fifty children, had just killed and were in the process of skinning hundreds of bison when they were attacked by a force of a thousand Sioux warriors. More than seventy Pawnees were killed, including some of their leading chiefs and many women and children. The victorious Sioux took all their horses and meat. The Pawnees staggered back to their villages and within two years they had made the move to Indian Territory, leaving behind their cherished homeland.

The Indian Office's response to the widespread violence and the relentless American demand for Indian lands was to intensify the reservation policy: the objective, as Commissioner of Indian Affairs Francis Walker put it in 1872, was to "make the Indians as comfortable on, and uncomfortable off, the reservations" as possible. As part of what became known as the "Peace Policy," treaty councils were held with the Kiowas, Comanches, Cheyennes, and Arapahos at Medicine Lodge in Kansas in 1867 and with the Sioux and Arapahos and, separately, with the Crows at Fort Laramie, Wyoming in 1868. The Fort Laramie council was captured in an early photograph (fig. 10) and also in the winter counts of Lone Dog, described as "many flags were given them by the Peace Commission," and Baptiste Good, entitled "Baptiste-Good-made-peace-with General Harney-for-the-people winter" (fig. 11). The latter, showing a handshake between an Indian and an officer, may be a case of self-aggrandizement on the part of Baptiste Good: he was not one of the twenty-five Brule chiefs who put their marks on the treaty.

As a result of these treaties, the western Great Plains from Montana to the Rio Grande effectively passed into American hands. The treaties started with a declaration of peace between the United States and the Indians. They then specified

10. The U.S. view of the 1868 Fort Laramie Treaty Council: U.S. Army commissioners inside tent, 1868, Fort Laramie, Wyoming. National Archives, Smithsonian Institution. SPC Plains Dakota, BAE 24–29, 00514500.

reservations—"permanent homes"—for the Indians: in the north, the western half of South Dakota was reserved as the "Great Sioux Reservation" for the Sioux, and the Crows were given a reservation along the Yellowstone in southeastern Montana; in the south, two swaths of land in Indian Territory were put aside for the Kiowas and Comanches and the Cheyennes and Arapahos. The Indians were given annuities, some of which were to be expended on "citizens clothes"—suits for the men and boys, flannel skirts for the women and girls. The services of farmers, blacksmiths, and millers would be provided by the government to enable the transition to individualized allotments. The Indians pledged to "compel their children" to attend schools. This was the same assimilation policy that had been advocated by John Dougherty in 1829. While this supposed

11. Sioux views of the 1868 Fort Laramie Treaty Council: Lone Dog's Many flags were given them by the Peace Commission; Baptiste-Good-made-peace-with-General-Harney-for-the-people winter. Mallery, *Picture-Writing of the American Indians*, 285, 326.

transition to agricultural self-sufficiency was taking place, the Indians would be allowed to continue hunting on the ceded lands "so long as the buffalo may range there in such numbers as to justify the chase." This last clause was seen by the Indians as a continued right to the lands, but to the United States it was a completed cession that opened up the western Great Plains to Americans (fig. 9).

Some of the Indians did confine themselves to the designated reservations, but others mounted a furious resistance. On the southern Great Plains, the end came quite quickly when the Comanches, weakened by famine and the collapse of their century-old economic system, were cornered and defeated by the U.S. Army in Palo Duro Canyon in the Panhandle of Texas on September 28, 1874. The fifteen hundred or so surviving Comanches were rounded up and driven to their reservation at Fort Sill.

On the northern Great Plains, the strong resistance by the Sioux and their allies, led by inspired chiefs like Sitting Bull and Crazy Horse, and including the decisive victory at the Little Big Horn on June 25, 1876, was overcome by a brutal campaign of total war, targeting especially the Indians' winter camps. With their leaders scattered and dead, and their staff of life—the bison—cut out from under them, the Sioux capitulated. By 1881 all their bands had withdrawn into the Great Sioux Reservation.

By that time, the Great Sioux Reservation had already been diminished by the Black Hills cession of 1877. The sacred Black Hills—Paha Sapa to the Sioux—had been overrun by Americans, a clear violation of the 1868 Fort Laramie treaty, following the discovery of gold there in 1874. The United States offered to buy the now-valuable Black Hills, but the Sioux refused. So the United States, in effect, annexed Paha Sapa and the rest of western South Dakota. Even by the standards of American self-serving legal parameters, this was an unjust taking: the 1868 Treaty of Fort Laramie had specified that no further changes could be made to the reservation boundaries without the assent of three-quarters of the adult male Sioux; fewer than 10 percent of the adult males signed on to 1877 cession, and many of them did so because they were bribed. Congress immediately enacted a statute that legitimized the fraudulent treaty. The Black Hills were gone, but the loss has never been accepted by the Sioux, even to this day.

The massacre at Wounded Knee on December 29, 1890, when a panicked Seventh Cavalry killed 250 Sioux and buried 146 of them in a mass grave on the snow-covered plains (fig. 12), is often seen as the end of the Indian wars. But really, it was a final reverberation of a resistance that had ended a decade earlier. The Ghost Dance, a messianic merger of Christianity and traditional beliefs, had reached the Sioux in 1889. It promised a return to a better time, when there were plentiful bison and no Americans. The singing of Ghost Dance songs

12. Gathering of the dead at Wounded Knee. Courtesy of the Nebraska State Historical Society. RG 2845. PH-13-10.

in an atmosphere poisoned by tension provoked the massacre, which stands as a horrifying symbol of a horrifying century of dispossession for the Plains Indians.

And the dispossession continued. In fact, the Wounded Knee Massacre took place on Pine Ridge Reservation, one of the five separate Sioux reservations that had been retained after the break-up of the Great Sioux Reservation in 1889 that opened up much of central South Dakota to settlers. The Sioux signed on to this after being told by the commissioner of Indian Affairs that they would "never get any better terms" than he was offering.

A similar compression of Indian space occurred in Montana at about the same time. In 1874 the Great Northern Reservation, embracing all the plains of Montana north of the Missouri and Marias Rivers, had been created as (again) a "permanent home" for the Blackfeet, Gros Ventres, and Assiniboines. The remainder of their hunting lands passed to the United States without payment. Fourteen years later, the Indians sold the fifteen million acres of the Great Northern Reservation for a payment of 28.7 cents an acre. They had no option but to sell. Their world had changed abruptly in 1883 when the last bison herds in their country were exterminated. Montana cattlemen lobbied for the dissolution of the reservation, using the familiar argument that the Indians had more land than they needed and were not using it to its fullest potential. Smaller reservations were retained at Fort Belknap, Fort Peck, and, for the Blackfeet, in the far northwestern corner of the Montana plains, where they meet the Rocky Mountains. In 1895 the Blackfeet were obliged to sell the western part of their reservation, the majestic country that in 1910 would become Glacier National Park. It was the same story of starving Indians selling their land, their only remaining resource, for a poor living on government annuities.

The dispossession of the Plains Indians would continue in the twentieth century, but it took a different form. On February 8, 1887, Congress passed the General Allotment Act, the final push to force Indians onto allotments. Every Indian head of family would be given 160 acres, and smaller acreages would be assigned to single adults and minors. In areas suitable only for grazing rather than farming, the size of the allotment was doubled. When all the allotments had been allocated, the remainder of the reservations, the "surplus lands," would be sold to Americans. The eastern reformers, "friends of the Indians," who were behind this legislation saw it as a means of transition to a bright future, with Indians living as yeoman farmers and fully incorporated into American society (albeit on the bottom rung of the social ladder). But as usual the gap between the rhetoric and reality was wide, and in time most of the allotments also passed into the hands of Americans.

CHAPTER FOUR

Against All Odds

In 1900 it seemed that the Plains Indians had no future at all and that their 13,500-year-long occupancy of the Great Plains was coming to a close. Some tribes were hovering on the brink of extinction, Indian cultural identities were still under attack through assimilation policies, and the loss of lands through the allotment program was in full swing. It was generally accepted at the time that Indians were "running out as a race."

But against all odds they survived. Their populations rebounded in the early decades of the twentieth century and have continued on an upward trajectory right up to the present. On the Great Plains, reservations are now islands of population growth in a sea of rural population decline.

The contrast between the young and rapidly growing populations of Plains Indians and the aging and stagnating populations of much of the Great Plains in general is clearly shown on a 2010 population pyramid comparing the entire population of Montana with that of the Northern Cheyenne Reservation located in southeastern Montana (fig. 13). The broad base of the Northern Cheyenne half of the pyramid, with 44.2 percent of the population under the age of nineteen, ensures that growth will continue, as these young people enter the childbearing years. The narrow base of the overall Montana pyramid, with only 25.3 percent of the population under the age of nineteen,

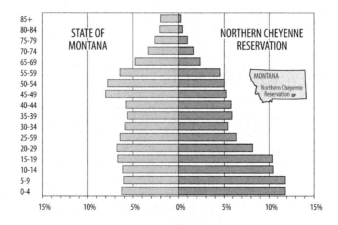

13. Comparison of Montana and Northern Cheyenne Reservation populations, 2010. Source: U.S. Census Bureau, 2010; Northern Cheyenne Tribe. Created by Ezra J. Zeitler.

indicates a population with little potential for growth. Young people, seeking economic and social opportunities elsewhere, leave, taking their child-bearing potential with them. Note also the much smaller numbers of Northern Cheyennes over the age of fifty (18.9 percent compared to 37 percent of Montanans in general), the result of poor living conditions and associated higher death rates. Still, the Indians' high birth rates offset the high death rates and guarantee that Indians will have a greater share of Great Plains population in the future.

There have also been victories in the courts, such as the Winters Doctrine (1908), emerging from a case involving the Gros Ventres and Assiniboines of the Fort Belknap Reservation in Montana, which affirmed that water rights were reserved for the Indians when their reservations were established. There were victories in Congress too, including the Native American Graves Protection and Repatriation Act (1990), which mandated the return of human remains and sacred items from museum shelves to their rightful owners. Some Indians have become relatively rich from the proceeds of casino gaming, and some reservations have resources—oil, coal, gas—that bring the promise of wealth. And throughout the twentieth century, Indians have come out from the Great Plains to excel in (these are historian Philip Deloria's words) "unexpected places" in mainstream culture: these include athletes like Jim Thorpe (Sauk and Fox) and Billy Mills (Oglala Sioux), artists like Oscar Howe (Yanktonai Sioux), dancers like Maria Tallchief (Osage), and acclaimed writers like N. Scott Momaday (Kiowa), James Welch (Blackfeet and Gros Ventre), and Louise Erdrich (Turtle Mountain Chippewa).

This triumph of survival was hard-earned through resistance and adaptation. It was achieved despite the discrimination, dispossession, and marginalization that continued to plague the lives of Plains Indians. A better future, when Plains Indians will thrive, not just survive, remains a battle to be won.

Twentieth-Century Dispossession

The more or less mandatory assimilation policy introduced by the General Allotment Act of 1887 operated until 1934, when it was repealed during the reform-minded administration of Commissioner of Indian Affairs John Collier, who stressed Indian self-determination and incorporation of Indians into American society as distinct communities, and on their own terms. In 1895 the Curtis Act extended the allotment policy to Indian Territory. Everywhere across the Great Plains in the 1890s and early twentieth century, the "mighty pulverizing engine" of allotments (this is President Theodore Roosevelt's metaphor) broke up the "tribal mass." Voluntary assimilation hadn't happened, so it was spatially imposed via the fragmenting of Indian communal lands.

In a laudable attempt to forestall the sale of allotments to non-Indians, the General Allotment Act stipulated that the federal government would hold the Indians' allotment titles in trust for twenty-five years. This was to the Indians' advantage for another reason: Indians did not have to pay taxes on their allotments until they actually owned them. However, the leasing of trust allotments was allowed in 1891, and the vast majority of Indians, not wanting to farm (or not able to because they lacked the means), gained a small income by allowing non-Indians to farm, graze, and mine their lands.

As demands for Indian lands intensified after 1900, the government's trust period was abridged. In a development that was formalized in the Burke Act of 1906, Indians who were declared "competent" could apply for immediate title to their allotments and then do with them as they pleased. What they mostly did was sell to land-hungry Americans. By the end of allotment in 1934, nationwide, the Indians' land base had been reduced from 138 million acres to 52 million acres through the sale of surplus lands and allotments. On the Great Plains, where reservations were often large and Indian populations still small from a century of dying (so there generally was a large amount of surplus lands after the allotments were allocated), the proportion of territory lost through this incremental dispossession was even greater. Two case studies—the Omahas in Nebraska and the Sisseton and Wahpeton Sioux of the Spirit Lake Reservation in North Dakota (formerly the Fort Totten, or Devils Lake Sioux, Reservation)—serve to reveal how Plains Indians continued to lose control of their lands in the twentieth century.

The Omahas were initially fortunate in their allotment experience. They had always been well regarded by the Indian Office as an accommodating people—peaceful, successful farmers and with a substantial progressive component who saw the advantages of assimilation, or at least the impossibility of continuing to live in traditional ways. This concession to necessity was recognized by one of the fifty-five Omahas who petitioned for allotment of their reservation in 1882:

> The road our fathers walked is gone, the game is gone, and white people are all around us. There is no use any Indian thinking of old ways; he must now go to work as the white man does. We want titles to our lands so that the land may be secure to our children.

The Omahas also had, in the person of anthropologist Alice Fletcher, a champion who was determined to get their reservation allotted so that they would not suffer the fate of their relatives, the Poncas, who had been marched out to Indian Territory in 1877. Fletcher lobbied tirelessly on the Omaha's behalf in Washington DC and was largely responsible for the act of August 7, 1882, that arranged for the sale of the southwestern corner of their reservation to finance the move to allotments. All of the remaining reservation lands were allotted, with 160 acres going to the head of every family, 80 acres to every single adult and orphan, and 40 acres to every other Omaha under the age of eighteen. In an exceptional clause, the Omahas were allowed to retain their surplus lands for future allocation to children born during the twenty-five-year trust period. This was one of the first reservations to be allotted in the United States.

The single-minded Fletcher set up a tent on the reservation and had each Omaha sign, or mark, an allotment certificate in front of witnesses. Contrary to her hopes, most Omahas, still looking to the past, chose land in the dissected, thin-soiled, wooded eastern portions of the reservation, where they were used to camping and socializing, rather than on the fertile plains to the west that were more suited to commercial agriculture. By 1884, 76,810 acres had been allotted to 1,194 Omahas, leaving

55,000 acres to be held in common for future allotments. As part of the agreement, the Omahas were "released" from federal supervision, except for the continued services of an agent and schoolteachers. It was, as their agent put it, "an experimental test of the capabilities of Indians to take care of themselves."

Subsequent developments show that the Omahas failed this test. By 1904, according to their agent, the Omahas, once self-sufficient hunters and farmers, were living entirely on leasing fees and annuities from past land sales and sinking rapidly into a state of "total demoralization."

By that time, the Omahas had already sold thirty-one thousand acres of allotments to surrounding Americans. Some of the buyers were farmers seeking to enlarge their holdings and reap economies of scale in a budding era of agricultural mechanization; others were speculators who bought the land, waited for values to rise, and then sold at a profit.

The process of selling allotments worked like this: owners of trust allotments petitioned the government for title, almost always with the objective to sell (otherwise, why take the land out of trust and have to pay taxes on it?); if the request was approved, a government appraiser would set the selling price; the allotment was then advertised for sale in local newspapers and on notice boards at the agency and sold to the highest bidder above the appraised value. It could be a complicated affair, because the allotments were often held by multiple owners, as a result of subdividing the land among inheritors. A majority of owners' signatures was generally sufficient to legitimize the sale.

By 1955, 103,515 acres of the Omaha reservation had been sold to non-Indians, leaving only 28,405 acres in Omaha lands. Much of this retained land was leased to non-Indians. Omahas continued to live on the leased lands, families crowded into ramshackle houses no bigger than sheds, set amidst fields of other peoples' crops. Only a handful of Omahas farmed on the reservation, and only one of them could support a family through his efforts. More than three-quarters of the reservation's families lived on less than $250 a year. Such was the legacy of allotment on the Omaha Reservation.

It was a similar story of quiet, relentless dispossession on the Spirit Lake Reservation in North Dakota, although unlike the Omahas, the Sisseton and Wahpeton Sioux also lost territory through surplus land sales. Their reservation, lying in the hills and rolling plains to the south of Devils Lake, was created in 1867. The next half century was a nightmare of poverty, sickness, and death. Tuberculosis and trachoma (a disease which, if untreated, results in blindness) were endemic. There was even an outbreak of smallpox in 1911, a terrifying visitation from the past. In many years, deaths outnumbered births: the reservation's Indian population of 930 in 1930 was lower than it had been in 1867. In their agent's opinion, the Devils Lake Sioux were "among the poorest and most unfortunately situated Indians" in the United States.

In 1904, over the objections of some of the Indians, the reservation was allotted in 160-acre plots: 1,193 Indians selected a total of 135,824 acres, leaving 92,144 acres of surplus lands, mainly on the outskirts of the reservation (fig.14). The surplus lands were completely sold by 1910, mainly to Scandinavian settlers who had poured into North Dakota in the late nineteenth century. By 1925 more than half of the allotments had also been sold. With the Indian population stagnant, and the non-Indian population growing, there were actually more Scandinavians than Sioux on the reservation by 1929.

This demographic situation was reversed after 1930, as Indian death rates declined with the introduction of basic health services (trachoma, for example, was virtually eliminated on the reservation by 1940), while birth rates remained high. At the same time, the non-Indian population of the reservation,

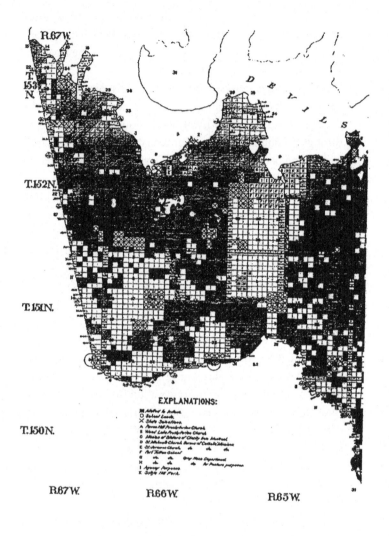

R.67 W.

T. 153 N.

T. 152 N.

T. 151 N.

T. 150 N.

DEVILS

EXPLANATIONS:

Allotted to Indians.
School Lands.
State Selections.
A Prairie Hill Presbyterian Church.
B Wood Lake Presbyterian Church.
C Sisters of Sisters of Charity from Montreal.
D St. Michaels Church. Bureau of Catholic Missions.
E St. Jeromes Church.   do   do   do
F Fort Totten School
G   do   do   Gray Nuns Department
H   do   do   do   for Pasture purposes.
I Agency Purposes.
K Sullys Hill Park.

R.67 W.   R.66 W.   R.65 W.

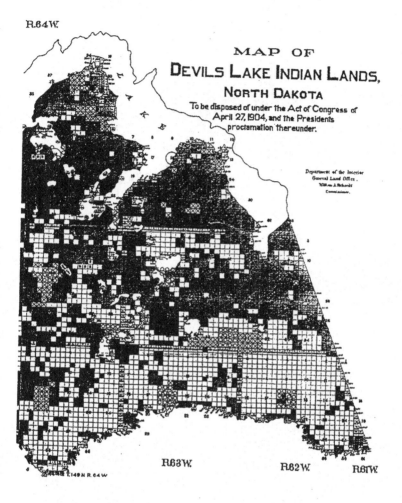

14. Allotments, Fort Totten Reservation, 1904. Reprinted from the
American Indian Culture and Research Journal 20, no. 2, by permission
of the American Indian Studies Center, U CL A. Copyright 1996, Regents
of the University of California.

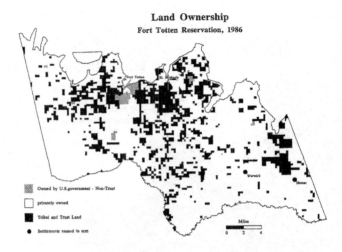

Land Ownership
Fort Totten Reservation, 1986

Owned by U.S. government - Non-Trust

privately owned

Tribal and Trust Land

● Settlements named in text

Miles
0   2   4

15. Indian lands, Fort Totten Reservation, 1986. Reprinted from the *American Indian Culture and Research Journal* 20, no. 2, by permission of the American Indian Studies Center, UCLA. Copyright 1996, Regents of the University of California.

like rural populations elsewhere on the Great Plains, began a protracted decline. By the 1990s, fully three-quarters of the reservation's population was Indian.

Meanwhile, the Indians' land base was steadily eroded through the sale of allotments. This loss of lands was reversed in a small way after the 1930s, but still, by 1986 three-quarters of the reservation's land was owned by non-Indians (fig. 15). Much of the retained tribal and individual trust lands were leased to non-Indians who lived elsewhere, giving the reservation's landscape an empty appearance.

This is a situation that prevails on many Great Plains reservations: a majority Indian population, but with the land predominantly owned by non-Indians. It is a complex geography, a patchwork pattern of ownership that greatly complicates issues such as hunting and fishing rights or jurisdiction over crimes within the boundaries of reservations.

This issue of sovereignty, involving who has the right to make the decisions in a given area, came to the fore on the Spirit Lake Reservation in the 1990s. It involved a dispute between the tribe and the state of North Dakota over the provision of electrical services to the reservation. The tribe wanted to contract with a private company, arguing that it was the most economical option and entirely within its rights on its own reservation; the state insisted that its Public Service Commission had the authority to regulate utilities throughout all of North Dakota. The case was heard in federal court in 1993.

The state emphasized the land ownership situation, claiming that the reservation had been "diminished" by the sale of surplus lands and allotments. In other words, according to the state, the reservation had "lost its Indian character," and therefore the Sisseton and Wahpeton Sioux had lost their sovereignty. The tribe countered by arguing that the population of the reservation was overwhelmingly Indian, and that burial places and other sacred sites were distributed throughout its length and breadth.

In his concluding statement, Judge Patrick A. Conway ruled that the Spirit Lake Sioux did have the right to contract for electrical services on Indian lands on the reservation, but not on those lands (the vast majority of the reservation) owned by non-Indians. The lawyers for the Spirit Lake Sioux declared this a major victory, but in truth the victory was Pyrrhic. The Indians' sovereignty had been moved from the reservation's exterior boundaries to interior boundaries enclosing only those lands held in trust by the tribe or individual members of the tribe.

This is not an isolated case of circumscribed Indian sovereignty on the Great Plains. To give another example, in 1998 the U.S. Supreme Court unanimously ruled that the Yankton

Sioux Reservation had been diminished in 1894 when its surplus lands were thrown open to Americans. Delivering the opinion of the court, Justice Sandra Day O'Conner said "the ceded lands no longer constitute 'Indian Country,'" and "the State now has primary jurisdiction over them." The state of South Dakota began showing only the diminished version of the reservation on its official road maps.

Clearly, the effects of the 1887 General Allotment Act did not end with the loss of Indian lands through surplus land and allotment sales, or even with the repudiation of the policy in 1934. Instead, they cast a long shadow into the present, compromising the Indians' sovereignty on their own reservations and perpetuating the history of dispossession.

That history took an even more blatant turn after the end of the Collier administration in 1945. In a time of national xenophobia, when no person or group could be seen to be less than 100 percent American and when conservatives wanted to strip the size of the federal government, the tide of sentiment in Congress swung back to Indian assimilation. Collier's self-determination efforts were labeled "communistic" and "un-American." Politicians (especially western politicians who resented the Indians' control of large swaths of land) now urged "the end of the guardianship responsibility" and "releasing the Indians from federal supervision." The result was a new policy that prevailed in the 1950s and 1960s and was aptly described by the ugly word *termination*.

In accordance with House Concurrent Resolution No. 108, passed by Congress on August 1, 1953, selected reservations would be abolished, the federal government would withdraw its oversight, and services would be taken over by the states and by the tribes themselves. Across the nation, from 1953 to 1962, 109 tribes and bands were terminated. The Poncas of Nebraska were one of these dematerialized tribes.

For such a small nation, the Poncas have a famous history. After being expelled from their reservation in what was then Dakota Territory in 1877, they endured terrible conditions on the forced march south to Indian Territory, and they continued to die in great numbers once they were there. On January 1, 1879, the Ponca chief Standing Bear and twenty-nine followers fled their new reservation and headed back to Nebraska. They reached the Omaha Reservation in mid-March, where Standing Bear was arrested for leaving Indian Territory.

What happened next is not only a great Indian story but also a great American story, a rare instance of Plains Indians being treated justly in the nineteenth century. In the widely publicized case *Standing Bear v. Crook*, heard in Omaha circuit court, an overtly sympathetic Judge Elmer Dundy ruled that Standing Bear was a "person" in the eyes of the law and entirely within his rights to withdraw from his tribe and from Indian Territory. Exonerated, Standing Bear became an early media hero, a symbol of the prevailing inhumanity of Indian policy.

Standing Bear's Northern Poncas (the Southern Poncas remained in Indian Territory) were given land in their old homeland along the Niobrara. They did well, and in 1881 their lands were recognized as a reservation. In 1891 their reservation was allotted, with 27,202 acres being divided among 167 heads of families and single adults, leaving 70,000 acres of surplus lands. These surplus lands were quickly sold. As was the case on other Great Plains reservations, they were first taken by speculators, who subsequently sold them at a profit to genuine settlers. Following the abbreviated trust period, almost all the allotments were sold too. By 1939, only 1,028 acres remained in Ponca hands, and by 1962, on the eve of termination, they retained a mere 834 acres.

Moreover, by that time most of the 442 Poncas no longer lived on the reservation but were scattered across eastern

Nebraska and the nation. In such a situation, it was impossible for the Poncas to maintain tribal cohesion. They were an easy target for termination.

On September 5, 1962, the Northern Poncas were terminated as a tribe. By a vote of 230 in favor and 22 opposed, they agreed to their own dissolution. It was a concession to a sad reality, as one of the Poncas, Peter La Claire, explained at the time:

> We want to terminate because there is nothing here. Our young men have all gone. They no longer care for farming like in the old days. They like city life. We have no housing, no work and little to do. So we want to see our tribal lands and buildings sold and divided before they tumble down.

The reservation's assets were assessed and divided up among the Poncas, each of whom received about $450. Without government services (the loss of health care was especially devastating) and with their tribal identity nullified, the Northern Poncas descended into abject poverty. By 1990, 52 percent of Indians in Knox County, Nebraska, where the Ponca Reservation had been located, were living below the poverty level.

But even as the Northern Poncas were being terminated, the pendulum of federal Indian policy was swinging back to self-determination. In an emerging era of civil rights, there was a new resolution, focused especially on education and economic development, to help Indians help themselves succeed in America's "Great Society." Eventually, all terminated tribes and bands that sought restoration were reconstituted, and federal supervision was put back in place.

On October 31, 1990, the Northern Poncas were resurrected as the Ponca Tribe of Nebraska. And although they were not allowed a new reservation, they were given fifteen hundred acres in the country of their origins to serve as a foundation for growth. They have since built on that foundation, setting up tribal headquarters in the town of Niobrara and tribal service centers at Norfolk, Lincoln, and Omaha, Nebraska, and Sioux City, Iowa. A glance at their official website listing scheduled activities for a few days in June 2014 shows a sweat lodge in Omaha, a circle of elders meeting in Sioux City, a talking circle in Lincoln, and a powwow committee meeting in Norfolk. The two thousand or so Poncas of Nebraska, like other Plains Indians, are still poor, but they have come a long way since the dark days of termination.

There was a related aspect of termination, concerning Indian claims against the United States, that deeply involved Plains Indians in the decades after the Second World War. It hadn't been easy for Indians to lodge claims against the government. After 1863 they were specifically barred from doing so, unless they first obtained permission via a jurisdictional act of Congress. This was a drawn-out process. It took the Pawnees, for example, almost thirty years to get an award compensating them for surplus lands that had been taken without payment when their reservation in Indian Territory was allotted in 1892. By 1945 the backlog of unresolved claims was enormous.

In 1946 the Indian Claims Commission was created to remedy this situation. For humanitarians like Felix Cohen, the preeminent authority on Indian law at the time, the Indian Claims Commission was a moral necessity, a chance for the United States to finally give the Indians their "day in court." For the assimilationists, it was an opportunity to "clean the slate" of outstanding claims as a prelude to terminating the reservations and getting the government out of the "Indian business." As the commission itself curtly wrote in its final report in 1978, "the problem of giving the Indian his due had to be balanced somehow with giving him his walking papers."

Eighteen Great Plains nations, from the Blackfeet in the north to the Lipan Apaches in the south, registered claims relating to the past injustices of federal Indian policy. These included claims for lands taken illegally, "unconscionably low" payments for Indian lands, and the government's misuse of Indian monies. Here, perhaps, was a possibility of achieving "belated justice."

Indian Claims: Belated Justice?

The Indian Claims Commission was composed of three (later four) judges appointed by the president. Most of the judges had no background in Indian law, and until 1969, when Bradley Blue, a Lumbee Indian, was appointed, the commission lacked an Indian presence. The commission functioned as a court that heard the arguments of two adversaries—the Indian claimants and the United States as defendant—and then passed judgment. Awards were monetary only; return of land was expressly excluded.

In a typical claim involving land, the Indian claimants first had to prove that they had held title to a specific territory. This could be done by establishing "original title"—by proving that they had "exclusively occupied" a defined area "since time immemorial." Or they could prove that they had held "recognized title," meaning that the government, in taking Indian lands, had acknowledged that a particular area belonged to a particular tribe. Recognized title, unlike original title, gave the Indians' land the status of private property protected by the Fifth Amendment to the Constitution, a crucial difference when it came to awards.

Once title to the land was established, the proceedings moved to the valuation stage. Here the Indian claimants had to demonstrate that the original payments for the land were significantly below its "fair market value," or what an "informed purchaser" would have paid for it "at the time of taking" (subsequent developments, such as the discovery of oil, could not be taken into account). The difference between the original payments and the fair market value, minus lawyers' fees and "gratuitous offsets" (or past payments made to the Indians without obligation, as in the form of emergency rations), constituted the new award. Once an award was accepted and the case dismissed, the case was dead forever, and the Indians' day in court was over.

The Pawnees were one of the first tribes to lodge a claim with the commission (in 1947), and their experience was largely representative of other Plains Indians' claims cases. The fact that the Pawnees did not receive their award until 1964 stands as testimony to the complexity of the process. The Pawnees were requesting an award of about $30 million for almost forty million acres of the central Great Plains that had been sold to the United States in the nineteenth century for an "unconscionable consideration," payments "so small as to shock the conscience." They also registered smaller claims for fragments of reservation lands in Nebraska and Indian Territory that had been taken, they maintained, without their consent.

Like all Indian claimants, the Pawnees hired expert witnesses to make a case on their behalf, arguing that they had held title to the largest possible amount of land. The government's expert witnesses countered by arguing that the Pawnees had only exclusively occupied a small territory around their villages in central Nebraska. Also like many other Indian claimants, the Pawnees were represented by a lawyer who had little experience in Indian affairs. The government, on the other hand, had seasoned attorneys familiar with Indian law at their disposal. Given this discrepancy, it is hardly surprising that in 1950 the commission rejected all the Pawnees' major claims on the grounds that they had failed to prove title to their ancestral lands. Instead of receiving an award of $30 million, they were granted only a few hundred dollars for the small acreages that had been inappropriately taken from their reservations in Nebraska and Indian Territory.

The Pawnees immediately appealed the case to the Court of Claims, the appellate court for the Indian Claims Commission. The Court of Claims, taking its role seriously, lambasted the commission for making hasty and uninformed decisions, stating that the facts presented in the case were "entirely inadequate to form the basis for a just, equitable, and final settlement." The Court of Claims put its investigative staff to work and unearthed a "vast amount" of relevant information that had not been taken into account. They referred the case back to the commission and told it to do its job properly.

By this time, 1955, the Pawnees had hired more effective lawyers. Also, as the litigation before the commission accumulated, new operating procedures emerged. By the process of stipulation, claimants were permitted to agree to compromise territorial boundaries with other claimants so that the prerequisite of "defined areas" could be met. So the blurred picture of overlapping claims, with indefinite acreages and indistinct boundaries, was brought into sharp focus by "stipulation." Ironically, this was a distortion of historical reality: the border zones where Indian territories had merged and fluctuated were narrowed into hard and fast lines, often straight lines following no natural features, in order to satisfy the requirements for proving Indian title. As a result, the Indian Claims Commission concluded in 1957 that the Pawnees had proven Indian title to about twenty million acres on the central Great Plains.

The case then moved to the valuation stage. Again the Indian claimants and the government defendant, with their batteries of attorneys and expert witnesses, took stances in opposition to each other. The Pawnees claimed that they had been paid only about $1 million for their nineteenth-century cessions; the government proposed that the figure was more like $5 million. The Pawnees maintained that the ceded lands had a fair market value of $34 million; the government, calling the Pawnees' accounting "inflated" and "absurd," responded with a fair market value of $5 million. When the commission handed down its decision on June 14, 1960, its estimates of payments and fair market value were much closer to the government's figures than to the Pawnees'. Still, the commission did recognize that the original payments for their lands had been "unconscionably low," and it awarded the Pawnees $7,925,657.

A minimal amount of gratuitous offsets was deducted from the award, and a much larger amount, $876,897, went to the tribe's attorneys. In August of 1964, seventeen years after they had filed their claim, the Pawnees received $6,439,088 as a settlement for "past injustices."

The Pawnees, like every other Plains tribe that received a settlement, then faced a dilemma: should the money be invested for the good of the tribe as a whole—in education, for example, or job training—or should it be divided up among all the enrolled members? Garland Blaine, head chief of the Pawnees, favored the former option, but he conceded this might not be equitable, because only 453 of the total population of 1883 Pawnees lived on the "old land" in Oklahoma, with the remainder being distributed across twenty-eight states. Investment locally in the Oklahoma lands would benefit only a minority of the people. After much contentious debate (three of the council members resigned), the majority of the tribal council voted for distribution. In October 1964 each Pawnee received a payment of $3,530, which must have been a temporary boon to a poor people.

Other Great Plains tribes fought their individual battles before the Indian Claims Commission from 1946 until the commission finally closed its doors in 1978. Overall, the commission recognized that the American Great Plains north of Oklahoma had a fair market value of eighty-eight cents an acre when it was taken from the Indians, almost nine times the ten cents an acre that had originally been paid for the area. The largest award, just over $35 million, went to the Kiowas, Comanches, and Apaches in 1974 for their lands on the southern Great Plains. Other large awards were paid to the Cheyennes and Arapahos for eastern Colorado and adjacent Wyoming, Nebraska, and Kansas ($15 million) and to the Crows for their Yellowstone and Powder River country (just over $10 million).

The smallest award, $2,458, was made to the Poncas in 1965 for an accounting claim. The Poncas did, however, receive a measure of justice for their expulsion to Indian Territory in 1877. The commission acknowledged that the Poncas had held recognized title to their reservation, and that they had been illegally dispossessed, not just inadequately compensated. So they were not only awarded the difference between the original payment and the fair market value ($174,327) but also allowed 5 percent interest a year on the principal. When the award was actually made in 1972, it had accumulated to $1,013,425.

But as the Pawnee settlement showed, even large awards amounted to relatively small payments to individuals. The Yanktons, for example, each received $249 in 1960 after a decade of litigation before the Indian Claims Commission. That same year, the Omahas decided to divide most of their $2.9 million award (a second payment for the 1854 cession of northeastern Nebraska) among tribal members. In June 1962 each adult received a payment of $750. It was welcome relief in hard times, and bills were paid off, houses improved, and bicycles bought for the children (fig. 16). But it was quickly gone and hardly a settlement of "historical debts."

The Indian Claims Commission's work was widely praised, even by contemporary supporters of Indians like Felix Cohen, who thought then that "no nation on the face of the earth . . .

16. Omaha Indian children on new bikes, June 1962. Reprinted with Permission of the *Omaha World-Herald*.

has set itself so high a standard of dealing with a native aboriginal people." And it is true that the United States was decades ahead of other colonial societies, such as Australia and New Zealand, in considering indigenous claims.

But in many ways, the commission was more a continuation of the past than a break from it. As in the nineteenth century, it was a situation of poor people conceding to low monetary payments for their lost lands. These second payments were belated for sure, but hardly justice. At no stage of the litigation process was the value that the Plains Indians placed on their lands as homelands taken into account: as the Court of Claims bluntly expressed it in the Otoe and Missouria case, "values cannot be determined on the basis of berries and wild fruits."

One Great Plains nation, however, the Sioux, has not been willing to accept a payout for cherished lands that were forfeited in the nineteenth century. The Sioux claims case, involving the taking of the Black Hills in 1877, spanned almost sixty years. After going through the torturous process of obtaining a special jurisdictional act from Congress, the Sioux took their case to the Court of Claims in 1920, arguing that their lands had been taken without compensation and in violation of the Fifth Amendment. Their case was dismissed in 1942, so the Sioux resubmitted it to the Indian Claims Commission in 1946.

The commission agreed that the Sioux were entitled to a new compensation for the expropriation of the Black Hills. The area had been taken for almost nothing yet had a fair market value of $2.32 an acre, a high valuation because an informed purchaser in 1877 would have known very well that there was gold there. The total award came to $17.5 million. On appeal to the Court of Claims, their case was again dismissed on the grounds that the court's previous decision in 1942 barred any further action.

The Sioux persisted. In 1978 they obtained a special act from Congress to allow another hearing before the Court of Claims, without regard to its previous decisions. This time, the court supported the Sioux and ruled that the Black Hills had been illegally taken. The Sioux were due not only the principal of $17.5 million, but also 5 percent interest a year on that amount from 1877 on. Finally, in 1980, the Supreme Court confirmed that the 1877 cession had violated the earlier Treaty of Fort Laramie, which had put aside the Black Hills for the "absolute and undisturbed use and occupation" of the Sioux. By the time of the Supreme Court's decision, with interest accruing, the Sioux's award stood at $102 million.

But for many Sioux, no monetary award will ever be justice for the loss of the Paha Sapa. These, some of the poorest people in the United States, have resolutely refused to accept the money, which now amounts to about $1.3 billion. Theresa Two

Bulls, former president of the Oglala Tribe of Sioux, explained their stance: even this massive amount of money would not amount to much when divided among more than a hundred thousand Indians and would quickly be gone. "We're poor now," she said, "but we'll be poorer when that happens."

Instead, the Sioux want at least some of the Black Hills back. They don't want to dispossess others, but much of the Black Hills is federally owned, which raises the possibility of a benign return of some land. In 2014 this seems more feasible than ever; President Barack Obama has suggested that the matter could be settled in Congress if the nine nations of the Sioux could agree to a unified plan. Congress has returned land to Indians before (in 1970, in New Mexico, the revered Blue Lake was given back to the Taos Pueblo), so perhaps in the not-too-distant future, the Sioux's long road to justice will come to a good end in the sacred heart of their country.

Sacred and Profane Places

Throughout the Great Plains there are sacred places venerated by Americans in general—a myriad of churches and grave-yards and scenic landscapes like the last remaining preserves of tallgrass prairie, the unworldly Badlands, and the Black Hills themselves, sacred at least in a patriotic sense, with four presidents' faces carved on Mount Rushmore. But largely hidden from the American mainstream are innumerable places that are sacred to Plains Indians, an alternative, deeper geography going back centuries to a time before the land was squared off, claimed, and dug over.

Some of the sacred places are revered as the sites of the original creation, such as those laid down for the Blackfeet by Old Man on his journey through Montana and Alberta. Some are medicine wheels, circular rock structures that may be diagrams of the heavens. The Moose Mountain medicine wheel, for example, in Saskatchewan, is aligned to the summer solstice sunrise, and Wyoming's Bighorn medicine wheel, high in the mountains overlooking the plains, has six cairns on its perimeter that are oriented to where important stars rise at dawn. Many other sacred sites, including the Pawnees' Pa:haku, are retreats where particular rituals take place. Pawnee medicine men would go to Pa:haku each year to fast and dream and renew their healing powers. Even today, when Oklahoma Pawnees visit the old country in Nebraska, Pa:haku is one of their first priorities. The religions of Plains Indians are still lodged in sacred places and kept vibrant by performing ceremonies there, just as their ancestors did before them.

There is probably no Indian place on the Great Plains more sacred than Bear Butte in South Dakota. Many Plains tribes, from Canada to Texas, visit Bear Butte to pay their respects, but for the Sioux, Cheyennes, and Arapahos, especially, it is a sacred altar. This is where the Sioux were presented with the star map that subsequently oriented their spiritual life and where the mythic Cheyenne prophet, Sweet Medicine, received the four sacred arrows that are at the heart of their religious beliefs. To add to the power of the place, the great Sioux war chief and medicine man, Crazy Horse, was born near Bear Butte around 1840; undertook the *hanblecheyapi*, or "vision quest," there in 1871; and may well be buried in its sacred soil.

Bear Butte is a laccolith, a volcanic intrusion standing more than a thousand feet above the surrounding plains, just to the northeast of the Black Hills (fig. 17). Viewed from the ground, it resembles a sleeping grizzly bear. To the Sioux, Bear Butte is the sanctuary where the vision quest takes place. Young men, after a long period of preparation, including sweat lodges and instruction from a holy man, repair to Bear Butte, seeking a vision that would guide their lives. At Bear Butte, inside a scared circle of flags, tobacco ties, and sage, the young man fasts

17. Bear Butte. Courtesy of Kari Forbes-Boyte.

and humbles himself, hoping, as an old Sioux explained in an interview with geographer Kari Forbes Boyte in 1996, to "see dreams that are real, dreams that have survived the generations." The vision seeker then descends the cosmic mountain, and the holy man who had prepared him helps to interpret what he has seen. This knowledge is not just for the individual but for the benefit of all the society: in the words of Sioux elder Nellie Red Owl, the vision seekers "pray for our food, for our children to grow strong. When they pray, God answers them."

Solitude is essential for the vision quest, but Bear Butte no longer provides it. Bear Butte is also a state park, run by South Dakota Game, Fish, and Parks with an operating philosophy of multiple use, including tourism. Bear Butte is now a prime example of how difficult it is for Indians to preserve the integrity of their sacred sites—and maintain the ceremonies that take place there—as the modern world crowds in all around.

As a state park, Bear Butte is open to all for recreational activities. Hiking trails cross the mountain, and observation platforms allow the scenery to be appreciated in all its grandeur. The observation platforms also afford access to the Indians' most sacred retreats, so much so that Sioux have been forced to pursue their vision quests elsewhere, in more remote locations. The connection between the ritual and the place has been compromised: as the Sioux holy man Richard Two Dogs explained in 1996, "The religion is rooted in the land. And you can't have religion without the land."

In 1982 the Sioux and Cheyennes brought suit in federal district court, claiming a right to unrestricted religious use of Bear Butte and demanding a discontinuation of any further development there. Despite nominal protection under the American Indian Religious Freedom Act (which had been passed by Congress in 1978 to secure Indian religions and holy sites), the unfavorable ruling in their case, *Fools Crow v. Gullet*, was that the Indians had not proven that Bear Butte was "central and indispensable to their religion." That ruling was confirmed upon appeal to the Court of Claims.

To its credit, South Dakota Game, Fish, and Parks has taken steps to accommodate the Indians' religious needs. It has built a trail exclusively for Indian worshippers, waived the entrance fee for those seeking to pray, and urged non-Indians to respect the sacred circles. But it is not enough: the agency's multiuse policy is just not compatible with the Indians' need for solitude. The Sioux have requested that the park be set aside for their exclusive use in June and July, the main months for the vision quest. But those, of course, are also the main tourist months, so the Indians' request is unlikely to be honored. One despairing Sioux expressed his fear that without the prayers the sacredness of Bear Butte will fade, until one day all that will be left are signs saying "Indians used to pray here."

The problem is not only competing land uses at the site but also commercial developments around Bear Butte that intrude on the silence and darkness of the mountain. The city of Sturgis, which attracts about a half million motorcyclists each August, is only a few miles away. Developers have put on rock concerts and have built bars, campgrounds, and vast parking lots on the fringes of Bear Butte. There are plans for a shooting range nearby, and, if approved, the sound of gunfire would echo up the mountain. There are prospects for oil drilling, and gas flares would illuminate the night and obscure the stars. To the Indians, all of these developments add up to the desecration of a profoundly sacred place.

Indian country is being desecrated in many parts of the Great Plains, and for every sacred site there is a profane site capitalizing on the Indians' poverty and despair. There are sites of mineral extraction that bring needed jobs but also tear up and pollute the land; there are sites where enterprises like toxic landfills and equally toxic hog "farms" are located, because no one else is desperate enough to want them nearby; and, perhaps the most egregious example of a profane place, there is Whiteclay, Nebraska, a settlement entirely premised on the sale of alcohol to Indians.

In the early twenty-first century, much of the northern Great Plains is in the midst of a mining boom. New techniques of hydraulic fracturing and horizontal drilling have unlocked buried treasures of coal, oil, and gas, both on and off reservations. The environmental side effects are extreme, from waste pits where the chemical effluents from the mining are stored, to overtaxed gravel roads that were never meant to carry convoys of large trucks, to once-pristine landscapes now bristling with oil derricks ten stories high. Plains Indians are faced with a tough choice between taking advantage of a rare economic opportunity or preserving the natural and spiritual integrity of their homelands.

The Crows and Blackfeet of Montana have recently opted for economic development based on coal and oil extraction. In 2008 the Crows entered into an agreement with an Australian company to develop a coal liquefaction plant that will yield taxes, royalties, and a share of the profits. To the north, in the lee of Glacier National Park, the Blackfeet have contracted with drilling companies to begin hydraulic fracturing on leased lands on their reservation, pumping solutions of sand, water, and chemicals into the geology to pry apart the rock beds and extract the oil. Their oil and gas manager, Grinnell Day Chief, representing one segment of the tribe, anticipated that "it'll change the lives of a lot of people. . . . It'll be a boost to everybody." But other Blackfeet see it differently. Pauline Matt, a member of a group of women who want to stop the drilling, warned that "it threatens everything we are as Blackfeet."

There is a similar conflict between traditional values, emphasizing respect for the land, and a chance for economic betterment through mining on the Northern Cheyenne Reservation in southern Montana. This is a typically poor Indian place, with an unemployment rate of 80 percent and a median family income of $23,679 in 2010 (barely half the national average). The pragmatic tribal chairman, Leroy Sprang, himself a retired coal miner, wanted to contract with drilling companies to extract methane gas from the reservation's coal beds: "We'll look at anything that can make a job," he said in 2009. But others in the tribe were opposed to what they saw as a betrayal of their responsibility to protect the land. They pointed to the prediction of Sweet Medicine that digging up the "black earth" would lead to the disintegration of the tribe. And, like their ancestors, they paid attention to the messages of their dreams. Gertrude Firecrow, aged sixty-eight, twice dreamed of "big machines ready to dig into the reservation." In her dream, she saw their lights coming toward her house, and she had the suffocating feeling of being cornered, of "having no place to go." These two visions for the future of the Northern Cheyenne Reservation will not easily be reconciled.

On the Rosebud Reservation, in southern South Dakota, a different type of land use conflict has divided the Upper Brule Sioux since 1998. That year, the tribal council, hoping to alleviate the desperate poverty of the reservation (in 2013, Todd County, which lies entirely within the Rosebud Reservation, was the fifth poorest county in the nation, as measured by per capita income), signed a contract with Bell Farms of North Dakota to build a hog farm (factory, really) on tribal trust land. The plan was to house almost a million hogs in two hundred steel barns, which would have made it the third largest hog farm in the world. Bell Farms was particularly attracted to this location by the abundant water available in the Ogallala Aquifer (it was estimated that the hog farm would consume 1.7 million gallons a day) and by the reservation's inherent sovereignty that would allow the company to sidestep South Dakota's ban on large-scale corporate farming. Earlier plans for a massive poultry factory and a six-thousand-acre landfill had been overturned by the concerted opposition of some tribal members. But in 1998 the tribal council, persuaded by the prospect of 230 new permanent jobs and the promise of 25 percent of the profits, pushed through the agreement with Bell Farms.

By March 2000, twenty-four sheds had been built, each housing two thousand hogs. But disillusionment with the project was growing as the environmental consequences, including the residual lagoons of liquid manure, became apparent. In new council elections in 2000, members who had supported the contract with Bell Farms were defeated. The new council voted to void the contract, and its right to do so was upheld in federal district court.

Bell Farms removed the last of its hogs in 2008, and it seemed that the Rosebud Sioux had won a victory over corporate power. But the issue is probably not dead. Like other reservations (and like less developed countries throughout the world), Rosebud remains an attractive location for noxious enterprises like hog farms: there is plentiful cheap labor, environmental regulations can be avoided, and the options for residents to support themselves in other ways are limited.

Reservations where alcohol is prohibited (since 1953 the decision to allow alcohol on reservations has been left up to each tribe) tend to attract settlements to their borders where that very product is provided. Whiteclay, Nebraska, which clings to the bottom of South Dakota's Pine Ridge Reservation like a leech, is such a place. A ramshackle, unincorporated settlement of fourteen people, Whiteclay has four liquor outlets that together sell the equivalent of 4 million twelve-ounce cans of beer each year, mainly to the Oglala Sioux of Pine Ridge. The liquor stores don't permit drinking on their premises, and until 2013 (except for a short period in 1970) Pine Ridge prohibited alcohol. The result is apparent in Whiteclay's landscape of despair—Indians, young and old, men and women, drinking in groups in the shade, or unconscious on the sidewalks and streets. This is as far from Bear Butte as you can get.

Whiteclay is also the main source for beer and malt liquor that is carried back in bulk to the reservation, which begins only 250 feet to the north. Few families, if any, on Pine Ridge are untouched by the damage of alcohol, including domestic abuse and other forms of violence, an eruption of teenage suicides, and a high incidence of fetal alcohol syndrome.

Whiteclay has served this mercenary function for a long time; it has no other reason to exist. The town emerged in 1904 (at first it was called Dewing), after a fifty-square-mile buffer that had been put in place in 1882 to keep liquor dealers at a distance from Pine Ridge was cancelled and opened to the American settlers (and speculators). Individual bootleggers had the business to themselves until the state of Nebraska issued four liquor licenses in the 1950s and the 1970s. For the most part, Nebraska has since washed its hands of Whiteclay, insisting that the alcohol sales there are legal and that the problem lies with alcohol abuse on Pine Ridge.

The blatancy of the exploitation in Whiteclay has made it a notorious place, with coverage in the national media and two hard-hitting documentaries, *The Battle for Whiteclay* (2008) and *Sober Indian | Dangerous Indian: A Story of Empowerment through Sobriety* (2014). The battle was taken to federal court in 2012, when the Oglalas sued the four liquor stores and their suppliers (Miller, Pabst, Molson, Coors, Miller-Coors, and Anheuser-Busch), claiming compensation for damages to the amount of $500 million. The case was dismissed for lack of legal grounds. The battle has also been taken to the streets, where activists, Indian and non-Indian, have marched in protest and blockaded the road back to the reservation (fig. 18). The protest became violent in 2013 when activists tried to stop the beer deliveries. This was the prelude to a momentous vote on Pine Ridge Reservation.

On August 13, 2013, after more than a century of prohibition, the Oglalas voted to allow the sale and consumption of alcohol on the reservation. The closeness of the vote—1,871 in favor of legalization and 1,679 against—shows how divided the people are on this issue. Supporters of legalization welcome the taking of responsibility into their own hands and the marginalization of the Whiteclay merchants. They argue that they will be able to capture new revenues from alcohol sales taxes and use them to build treatment centers: "I'm ecstatic," said tribal council member Larry Eagle Bull. "I'm so happy our tribe took the direction to move forward and make history." Opponents, like tribal president Bryan Brewer, fear the consequences of having alcohol even more readily available: "We know there will be more violence," he warned, "more women and children who will be abused." What will happen next in this benighted

18. Protest at Whiteclay, Nebraska, 1999. Courtesy of William Lauer, *Lincoln Journal Star*.

place is not clear, but with the society so polarized, it is sure to be a stern test for Indian self-determination.

Prospect

There is, of course, no single prospect for the diverse Plains Indians, just as there was no single past. Each nation will deal with its situation in its own way. Some will be cohesive and able to take advantages of opportunities to build a future; others will be hampered by poverty and factionalism and will find it difficult to thrive. Some reservations contain valuable mineral resources that have the potential to generate wealth; others have little more than marginal grazing lands. Reservations located in relatively densely populated areas will be able to reap profits from gaming enterprises; others, especially those on the thinly populated western Great Plains, have few people on hand to attract to their casinos. It is also likely that Plains

Indians will be affected to different degrees by global climate change (although as poor people, with little security and few options, they are all vulnerable): the 2014 National Climate Assessment predicts that temperatures will rise most appreciably in Montana and Wyoming, bringing more frequent drought to the reservations there. Indian country in Oklahoma is also likely to see increased numbers of dry days each year, intensifying competition for water, already a scarce resource.

However, and again as in the past, the diverse Plains Indians will be subject to a single federal Indian policy. At the beginning of the twenty-first century, the Obama administration has made it a priority to improve the "nation-to-nation relationship" between the United States and the tribes. President Obama has proposed an increase of $3 billion in support to Indian communities in his 2015 budget, mainly aimed at enhancing education and economic development. He speaks encouragingly of an emerging Indian middle class, and he favors giving Indians the means to accomplish effective self-determination. He has appointed Indians, including Plains Indians, to positions of leadership in his administration, and in June 2014, he became only the second president in office to visit a reservation, when he attended the annual Cannon Ball Pow Wow at Standing Rock Reservation in North Dakota (which contains the third poorest county in the nation).

This is promising, but there is no guarantee that an enlightened Indian policy will continue in the future. All it would take is a new spasm of American xenophobia, such as happened in the 1950s, and, paradoxically, the first Americans would again be cast as un-American. Combine this with a drive to downsize the federal government, and drastic policies like termination could reappear. There were suggestions of this in the early 1980s when President Ronald Reagan's secretary of the interior, James Watt, ominously referred to Indian reservations as "an example of the failure of socialism." Despite a measure of protection through legal precedents like the Winters Doctrine, Indians are still subject to the plenary power of Congress, and at the mercy of its whims.

There is, however, an important difference now that should give Plains Indians, and Indians everywhere, grounds for optimism. A rapidly growing Indian population, if it can be mobilized, adds up to political clout. Politicians, Democrats and Republicans alike, always on the lookout for votes, are paying heed to this expanding constituency. In 2012 grassroots campaigning on reservations helped Democrats win Senate races in Montana (where Indians now make up 6.5 percent of the voting age population) and North Dakota. In the build-up to the 2014 midterm elections, Democrats opened field offices on, or near, all seven Montana reservations. In Oklahoma, gaming revenue from more than a hundred casinos could provide the necessary financial backing to promote Indian candidates for national office. There is great opposition to overcome; as Deloria writes, there seems to be "an active hostility to the very idea of Indian wealth," and to Indian power. But this is a resurgent population, so much so that in the future it will be possible to see Indians not in unexpected, but in expected, places of influence and authority in the Great Plains and the nation.

BIBLIOGRAPHY

Abel, Annie Heloise, ed. *Chardon's Journal at Fort Clark, 1834–1839.*
  Pierre: State of South Dakota, 1932.
The Battle for Whiteclay. Directed by Mark Vasina. 2008.
Bray, Kingsley M. "Teton Sioux: Population History, 1655–1881." *Nebraska
  History* 75 (1994): 165–88.
Calloway, Colin G. *One Vast Winter Count: The Native American
  West before Lewis and Clark.* Lincoln: University of Nebraska
  Press, 2003.
Cohen, Felix S. "The Erosion of Indian Rights, 1950–1953: A Case Study
  in Bureaucracy." *Yale Law Journal* 62 (1953): 348–82.
Deloria, Philip J. *Indians in Unexpected Places.* Lawrence: University of
  Press of Kansas, 2004.
De Mallie, Raymond J., ed. *Plains.* Vol. 13 of *Handbook of North Ameri-
  can Indians,* edited by William C. Sturtevant. Washington D C:
  Smithsonian Institution, 2001.
Forbes-Boyte, Kari. "Litigation, Mitigation, and the American Indian
  Religious Freedom Act: The Bear Butte Example." *Great Plains
  Quarterly* 19 (1999): 23–34.
Gilmore, Melvin R. *Uses of Plants by the Indians of the Missouri River
  Region.* Lincoln: University of Nebraska Press, 1977.
Grinnell, George Bird. *Blackfoot Lodge Tales.* Lincoln: University of
  Nebraska Press, 2003.
Hämäläinen, Pekka. *The Comanche Empire.* New Haven: Yale University
  Press, 2008.
———. "The Rise and Fall of Plains Indian Horse Cultures." *Journal of
  American History* 90 (2003): 883–62.

Indian Claims Commission. *Final Report.* Washington D C: Government Printing Office, 1978.

Kappler, Charles J. *Indian Affairs: Laws and Treaties.* 5 vols. Washington D C: Government Printing Office, 1903–38.

Keen, Judy. "For Indian Tribes, Economic Needs Collide with Tradition." *USA Today,* March 3, 2009, http://usatoday30.usatoday .com/money/industries/energy/2009–03–03-reservation_N.htm.

Leighly, John, ed. *Land and Life: A Selection from the Writings of Carl Ortwin Sauer.* Berkeley: University of California Press, 1963.

Mallery, Garrick. *Picture-Writing of the American Indians.* Tenth Annual Report of the Bureau of Ethnology. 1888/89. Washington: Government Printing Office, 1893.

Momaday, N. Scott. "Personal Reflections." In *The American Indian and the Problem of History,* edited by Calvin Martin, 156–61. New York: Oxford University Press, 1987.

Moulton, Gary E. *The Definitive Journals of Lewis and Clark.* 13 vols. Lincoln: University of Nebraska Press, 1983–2001.

Nasatir, A. P. *Before Lewis and Clark: Documents Illustrating the History of the Missouri, 1785–1804.* Lincoln: University of Nebraska Press, 1990.

Northern Cheyenne Tribe. *Northern Cheyenne Reservation: Demographic and Economic Information.* www.cheyennenation.com.

Pielou, Evelyn C. *After the Ice Age: The Return of Life to Glaciated North America.* Chicago: University of Chicago Press, 1991.

Ritter, Beth R. "The Politics of Retribalization: The Northern Ponca Case." *Great Plains Research* 4 (1994): 237–55.

Royce, Charles C. *Indian Land Cessions in the United States.* Eighteenth Annual Report, Bureau of American Ethnography. Washington D C: Bureau of American Ethnology, 1899.

Secoy, Frank Raymond. *Changing Military Patterns on the Great Plains.* Locus Valley N Y: J. J. Augustin, 1953.

Sober Indian | Dangerous Indian. Directed by John Maisch. 2014.

Sundstrom, Linea. "Smallpox Used Them Up: References to Epidemic Disease in Northern Plains Winter Counts, 1714–1920." *Ethnohistory* 44 (1997): 305–43.

Tyrrell, Joseph B. ed. *David Thompson's Narrative of His Explorations in Western America, 1784–1812.* Toronto: The Champlain Society, 1916.

United States Census Bureau. *The American Indian and Alaska Native Population: 2010*. Washington D C: U.S. Department of Commerce, January 2012.

Wedel, Waldo R. "The High Plains and Their Utilization," *American Antiquity* 29 (1963): 1–16.

Welch, James. *Fools Crow*. New York: Viking Penguin Inc. 1986.

Weltfish, Gene. *The Lost Universe: Pawnee Life and Culture*. Lincoln: University of Nebraska Press, 1965.

Williams, Timothy, and John Eligon. "Pine Ridge Reservation Votes to End Alcohol Ban." *New York Times*, August 14, 2013.

Wishart, David J. "Compensation for Dispossession: Payments to the Indians for their Lands on the Central and Northern Great Plains in the 19th Century." *National Geographic Research* 6 (1990): 94–109.

———. ed. *Encyclopedia of the Great Plains Indians*. Lincoln: University of Nebraska Press, 2007.

———. "Land Ownership, Population, and Jurisdiction: The Case of the Devils Lake Sioux Tribe v. North Dakota Public Service Commission." *American Indian Culture and Research Journal* 20 (1996): 33–58.

———. "The Pawnee Claims Case, 1947–64." In *Irredeemable America: The Indians' Estate and Land Claims*, edited by Imre Sutton, 157–86. Albuquerque: University of New Mexico Press, 1985.

———. *An Unspeakable Sadness: The Dispossession of the Nebraska Indians*. Lincoln: University of Nebraska Press, 1994.

Wood, Raymond W., and Thomas D. Thiessen, eds. *Early Fur Trade on the Northern Plains: Canadian Traders Among the Mandan and Hidatsa Indians, 1783–1818*. Norman: University of Oklahoma Press, 1985.

INDEX

Page numbers in italic indicate illustrations.

government, 105–6; creation story of, 2, 36, 113; economic development of, 117–18; homeland of, 31, 61, 89–90; horses of, 20; missionaries with, 73; population decline of, 66; sacred sites of, 2, 36, 113; smallpox among, 70; subsistence patterns of, 5; trade of, 18, 70. *See also* Piegan Blackfeet Indians

Blackfeet Reservation, xii, 118

Black Hills, 11, 20, 25, 32, 36, 51, 86, 112–14

Black Kettle, 84

Black Robe. *See* De Smet, Pierre-Jean

blacksmiths, 76, 80–81, 86

Blackwater Draw, 3

Blaine, Garland, 109

blankets, 18

Blue, Bradley (Lumbee), 106

Blue Lake, 113

Bodmer, Karl, *39*

Bosnian war (1992–95), 67

bows and arrows, 12, 20–24, 43, 51–52. *See also* weapons

Boyte, Kari Forbes, 115

Bozeman Trail, 84

Bradbury, John, 46–47

Brazos River, 37

Brewer, Bryan, 121–22

British, 16–19, *17*, 22, 46, 53–54. *See also* Europeans

Brule Sioux Indians, xii, 85–86, 119–20. *See also* Sioux nation

buffalo chips, 11

buffalo jumps and pounds. *See* cliff driving

buffalo wallows, 11

Bureau of Indian Affairs. *See* Indian Office

burial sites. *See* cemeteries

Burke Act (1906), 94

Caddoan-speaking peoples, 35

California, xii

calumet ceremony, 55

calumus root, 51. *See also* roots

camels, 4, 6, 7

Campbell, Robert, 36

camps, 37–41, *39*, 44, 46, 59, 67, 88

camus roots, 39. *See also* roots

Canada, 16, 18, 60, 70, 113–14. *See also* Alberta

Canadian River, 37

Cannon Ball Pow Wow, 123

Cannonball River, 49–50

Canopus, 43–44. *See also* stars

caribou, 7

casinos, 93, 123, 124

Catholics, 73, 75–77

cattle, 61, 90

cedar, 51

cemeteries, 14, 34, 101. *See also* human remains; sacred sites

ceremonies. *See* culture, traditional

Chardon, Francis, 71–72

Chaui dialect, 74. *See also* languages

Cherokee Indians, 73, 77, 80

Cheyenne Indians: attack on, 84; on Bear Butte, 116; bison of, 49–50; economic development of, 118–19; land claim of, 110; life patterns of, 21;

tuberculosis, 72, 97. *See also* diseases
Turner, Frederick Jackson, 60
Turtle Mountain Reservation, xv
Two Bulls, Theresa, 112–13
Two Dogs, Richard, 116

unemployment, xv, 104, 117–20
Union Pacific, 84
United States: Clovis culture in, 3–4; displacement of Indians in, 37; mammoth extinction in, 6; racial composition of, xi–xii; westward expansion of, 29–37, 63–65, 76–77, 87. *See also* Americans
Upper Brule Sioux Indians, 119–20
Upper Republican society, 14
urban areas, xiv
U.S. Army, 80, *86*, 87–89
U.S. Bureau of the Census, 60
U.S. Census (2001), xi, *xiii*
U.S. Census (2010), *x*, xi–xvi, 91–92, *92*
U.S. Congress: on assimilation, 90, 102; on Indian claims, 105, 112, 113; on Indian religions, 116; on Indian rights, 64, 92–93, 124; on land payments, 80–81, 88
U.S. Constitution, 106, 112
U.S. government: and alcohol, 72–73; on allotment, 95; claims against, 105–13; Indian policy of, 59, 63–68, 76–91, 102, 123–24; inoculation by, 28, 70; land holdings of, 29–30, 60, 88, 113; peace treaties

of, 85–86, *87*; supervision of Indians, 35, 75–78, 96, 102–5. *See also* Americans; Indian agents
U.S. Senate, 124
U.S. Supreme Court, 101–2, 112. *See also* courts of law

villages: attack on Indian, 84; bison in, 48–49; dispersal of, 77; division of labor in, 57–58; establishment of, 13–15; leadership of, 56; life patterns in, 38, 41–47, 54–55; of Omahas, 46; of Otoes, 31; of Pawnees, 41–45, 47, 85; and reservation system, 61; Sioux domination of Missouri River, 25, 32; smallpox in, 26–27, 70–72; territories of, 32–34; trade in, 69–70
violence, xv, 72, 83–85, 120, 122. *See also* warfare
Virginia City M T, 84
vision quest, 114–16

Wahpeton Sioux Indians. *See* Sisseton and Wahpeton Sioux Indians
Walker, Francis, 64, 85
warfare: of Comanches, 16; effect on Plains Indians, 59; and horses, 21–24; against Indian resistance, 88–89, *89*; in Indian Territory, 35, 37; Lewis and Clark on, 24–25; missionaries' disapproval of,

74; over bison range, 84–85; and smallpox, 27–28, 32, 70–71; and trading, 69–70. *See also* disputes; violence

warriors, 40, 57

Washington D C, 35

water, transport of, 58

watermelons, 42, 44

water rights, 92

water sources: of Comanches, 37; competition for, 21; on Great Plains, 10–12; quality of, 36; travel to, 20, 44; villages near, 13–14, 34; winter camps near, 41

water use, 119, 123

Watt, James, 124

weapons, 21, 23. *See also* bows and arrows; guns

Wedel, Waldo, 10, 11

Welch, James (Blackfeet and Gros Ventre), 93

Westport inspection station, 72

Whiteclay N E, 117, 120–21, *122*

White Horse (Omaha), 61–63

White River, 13

whites. *See* Americans; Europeans; non-Indians

whooping cough, 72, 75. *See also* diseases

Wichita Indians, 15, 31, 35, 53

Winnebago Reservation, xv

winter counts, 26–27, *27*, 84–85, *87*

winters: bathing during, 52; camps during, 37–39, *39*, 41, 44, 46, 67, 88; in concept of time, 29; severity of, 5, 10, 12, 20, 48; sustenance for, 41, 84;

trade during, 52. *See also* climate; seasons

Winters Doctrine (1908), 92, 124

Wisconsin, 4

Wisconsin glaciation, 3–7

women: activities of Pawnee, 43; agricultural work of, 38, 42, 44, 47–48; clothing for, 86; in Clovis culture, 5; collection of prairie turnips, 10, 38; ethnic cleansing of, 67; gendered expression of, 57; and horses, 20, 22; manual labor of, 57–58; marriages of, 69; in Medicine Lodge ceremony, 40; mortality of, 58, 84, 85; personal hygiene of, 52; within social structure, 56–59, 67–68, 74. *See also* gender, third

wood. *See* timber

World War II, 105

Wounded Knee, 66, 88–89, *89*

Wyoming: archaeological evidence in, 9, 14; attack in, 84; climate change in, 5, 123; land claim in, 110; medicine wheel in, 114; treaty council in, 85, *86*, *87*; trees in, 11

xenophobia, 102, 123

Yanktonais Sioux Indians, 25. *See also* Sioux nation

Yankton Sioux Indians, 25, 82, 110. *See also* Sioux nation

Yankton Sioux Reservation, 101–2

Yellowstone River, 49, 69, 110

yucca, 52

IN THE DISCOVER THE GREAT PLAINS SERIES

Great Plains Indians
David J. Wishart

Discover the Great Plains, a series from the Center for Great Plains Studies and the University of Nebraska Press, offers concise introductions to the natural wonders, diverse cultures, history, and contemporary life of the Great Plains. To order or obtain more information on these or other University of Nebraska Press titles, visit nebraskapress.unl.edu.

CPSIA information can be obtained
at www.ICGtesting.com
Printed in the USA
LVOW13s0844051017
550857LV00001B/1/P